CW01084171

Boxing

What the Best Boxers Know about Training, Footwork, and Combinations That You Don't

Table of Contents

Introduction

Have you ever been amazed by professional boxers' speed, agility, and technique? What do they know about training, footwork, and combinations that you don't?

From hours of intense training and years of experience in the ring, these elite athletes have developed skills giving them a competitive edge. By learning from the best boxers, you, too, can develop these skills and take your boxing to the next level. This guide will walk you through the fundamentals of boxing, from footwork and stances to punches, defense tips, and pro combinations, to get you started on your journey to becoming an expert boxer.

From the ancient Greek Olympiad to today's pay-per-view extravaganzas, the history of boxing is a thrilling tale spanning centuries. This sport has seen legendary fighters, fierce rivalries, and momentous moments that have gone down in history. A walk through the annals of boxing history reveals how this brutal sport has evolved, from bare-knuckle brawls in the 1800s to the invention of boxing gloves, which made the sport less deadly. Boxing is constantly changing. It's a sport demanding discipline, skill, and endurance from its practitioners, striving to outwit opponents and deliver the perfect knockout blow.

With such a rich history, it's no wonder boxing continues to captivate audiences worldwide, even today. This easy-to-understand guide provides an overview of the origins of boxing. Once you understand the context, you can move on to the techniques and strategies used by modern-day boxers. You'll explore important topics, such as stances, guards, punches, combinations, defense tips, and heavy bag training. You learn about common mistakes to avoid as you embark on your boxing journey. Additionally, you'll pick up helpful sparring secrets from the pros and discover how to execute those pro combinations that make successful champions in the ring.

While the sport of boxing is a serious business, you don't need to take it too seriously. Even beginners can have a great time learning the basics and developing skills in this incredibly rewarding sport. All it needs is dedication, hard work, and the right resources. If you're ready to take the plunge and enter the world of boxing, lace up your gloves and get ready for an exhilarating journey that will keep you on the edge of your seat. This guide is an excellent starting point providing everything you need to start. So, what are you waiting for? Let's get ready to rumble.

Chapter 1: The Beginning

Have you ever cheered on boxers in the ring and wondered where the sport originated? Believe it or not, boxing has a rich history that dates back centuries. In the early days, boxing matches were brutal and lacked any regulation. Boxers fought with bare knuckles, with no rules, leading to gruesome injuries. However, new laws were enacted to protect fighters from serious harm as the sport grew in popularity.

Throughout the years, boxing has evolved into the exciting and dynamic sport people know and love today. So, let's lace up your gloves and step back in time to learn more about the origins of boxing. This chapter provides a brief overview of the history and evolution of boxing, starting with its ancient roots. It highlights some of the most iconic boxers in history and their lasting legacies. By the end of the chapter, you'll better understand why boxing has become such a trendy sport.

The Fascinating Origins of Boxing: Unraveling Its Ancient Roots

Boxing has evolved in various ways over thousands of years, leading to different styles enthusiasts still practice. From gladiators in Ancient Rome to bare-knuckle fights in the 19th century, boxing has a fascinating history. This section examines the charming story of how this sport originated and its many transformations throughout history.

Ancient Egypt and Greece

Ancient Greek boxers depicted on a vase.
Antimenes Painter, CC BY 2.5 <https://creativecommons.org/licenses/by/2.5>, via Wikimedia Commons: https://commons.wikimedia.org/wiki/File:Boxers_Panathenaic_Met_06.1021.51.jpg

The rich history of this fantastic sport has its roots in the ancient civilizations of Egypt, Greece, and Rome. The Greeks practiced boxing as early as the 7th century BC. It quickly became one of the most popular sports in their culture, with athletes competing in local and national competitions. The sport was steeped in mythical symbolism and was an allegory for the hero's journey. Ancient Egyptian art depicts bare-knuckle fighting contests, one of the earliest boxing forms. These fights were brutal and often ended in death, as there were no rules, gloves, or weight classes. Instead, the fighters wrapped their hands in cloth or leather, leading to the development of the first boxing gloves.

Roman Boxing

When it was introduced to the Roman Empire, boxing transformed from a sport for entertainment to a means of protection - mercenaries and soldiers engaged in fistfights to keep in shape and test their fighting abilities. As Roman influence expanded, so did boxing, and it became a regular feature in their athletic competitions, known as the gladiatorial games. These games brought together the bravest and strongest fighters from across the empire, with large crowds gathering to witness this dangerous and deadly sport.

Earliest Evidence

The earliest evidence of boxing comes from ancient Sumeria, around 3000 BC, where people wrapped their hands in leather strips for protection. At first, it was a simple form of combat, but the sport became more structured and refined through its evolution. In ancient Greece, boxing became popular during the Olympic Games in 688 BC, one of the most prestigious events. The boxers wore leather gloves with metal or lead studs to inflict more damage on their opponents. The matches were brutal, often ending with serious injuries or death.

Transformation of the Sport

In the early 18th century, boxing transformed England. The sport became more organized with the Rules of Boxing in 1743, which established weight classes, banned biting and gouging, and standardized gloves. The first recognized heavyweight champion was the English bare-knuckle boxer James Figg, who dominated the sport in the early 1700s. He established a boxing school training young fighters who later became champions.

Recent Developments

The first modern boxing match occurred in 1867 between John Sholto Douglas, the Marquis of Queensbury, and John Graham Chambers, the founder of the Amateur Athletics Club. The match followed the Marquis of Queensbury's rules, which included a three-minute round, gloves, and a ten-second count for knocked-down fighters. These rules revolutionized the sport and made boxing more accessible to the masses.

Modern Day

Boxing continued to evolve throughout the ages and reached its modern form during England's 18th and 19th centuries. The English added further innovations, such as rounds, weight classes, and the traditional Queensberry rules still used today. In addition, boxing became more organized and was no longer confined to a particular style or social structure. From its humble beginnings as a brutal sport, boxing has come a long way and is one of the world's most beloved sports.

Many famous fighters emerged throughout the 20th century, such as Muhammad Ali, Joe Frazier, and George Foreman. These fighters brought new skills, strategies, and techniques to the sport, making it more entertaining and popular worldwide. However, the emergence of Floyd Mayweather Jr. - considered one of the best fighters of all time -

forever changed the boxing world. His record-breaking winnings and undefeated streak made him a legend.

Boxing has come a long way since its humble beginnings. From a primitive form of combat to a sophisticated sport with strict rules and regulations, it has dominated the sports arena worldwide. The first boxers paved the way for modern-day champions who have brought fame, glory, and entertainment to the sport. Boxing continues to evolve, and the world can look forward to more exciting matches and legendary fighters in the future.

Boxing in the Common Era: A Legacy of Greatness

From the first fights in ancient Greece to the present day, boxing has always been a physical and mental test of strength, endurance, and skill. The Common Era of boxing produced some of the greatest athletes and most unforgettable moments in sports history. From the golden age of Muhammad Ali and his rivalry with Joe Frazier to the recent triumphs of Floyd Mayweather Jr. and Manny Pacquiao, boxing remains a source of inspiration and awe for millions of fans worldwide.

The Common Era of boxing, known as the *modern era,* started in 1910, when the first heavyweight champion, Jack Johnson, was dethroned by Jim Jeffries in a racist and controversial bout. This era saw the rise of iconic fighters, such as Joe Louis, Rocky Marciano, Sugar Ray Robinson, and Muhammad Ali, who dominated their divisions and transcended the sport through their charisma, courage, and social impact.

Joe Louis, known as the Brown Bomber, reigned as heavyweight champion for a record-breaking 12 years and became a hero to Black and White fans for his sportsmanship and patriotism. Rocky Marciano, the only undefeated heavyweight champion in history, was a relentless and powerful fighter who retired at the peak of his career to preserve his legacy. Sugar Ray Robinson, considered by many experts the greatest pound-for-pound boxer of all time, dazzled his opponents and fans with his speed, technique, and showmanship.

Muhammad Ali, born Cassius Clay, was a boxing legend, cultural icon, and political activist. He won three heavyweight titles and fought some of history's most epic and controversial matches, including his

1964 upset of Sonny Liston, his 1971 defeat of Joe Frazier in the Fight of the Century, and his 1974 Rumble in the Jungle (in Zaire, Africa) against George Foreman. Ali's charisma, humor, and eloquence made him a beloved figure worldwide, and his stand against the Vietnam War and his advocacy for civil rights inspired millions of people.

The common era of boxing saw the emergence of many other great champions and rivalries, such as Julio Cesar Chavez, Mike Tyson, Oscar De La Hoya, Roy Jones Jr., Lennox Lewis, Evander Holyfield, Bernard Hopkins, and Manny Pacquiao. These fighters showcased different styles, personalities, and legacies, but all shared a passion for the sport and a desire to push themselves to the limit.

Today, boxing continues to evolve and adapt to new challenges and opportunities. The rise of MMA, digital media growth, and the pandemic have affected how the sport is watched and consumed, but the core values and excitement of boxing remain intact. The current champions and prospects, such as Canelo Alvarez, Anthony Joshua, Terence Crawford, Gennady Golovkin, Ryan Garcia, and Teofimo Lopez, are carrying on the legacy of greatness that boxing has fostered for over a century.

Boxing in the present era is not just a sport but a testament to human resilience, creativity, and excellence. The fighters who have graced the ring in this era have set the bar high for future generations and inspired fans to dream big and fight hard. So, whether you are a casual viewer or a diehard fan, boxing offers something for everyone who loves a good challenge, a good story, and great shows.

The following section dives deep into the fighters' stories that made this era so special. So, come, it's time to get ringside.

Muhammad Ali

Muhammad Ali is one of the greatest boxers ever – and for good reason. He won the world heavyweight champion title three times and was known for his unique fighting style, wit, and charisma. Ali was a lightning-fast fighter who "floated like a butterfly and stung like a bee." In addition, he was a civil rights activist who stood up for his beliefs regardless of the consequences. Ali retired in 1981 but remained iconic in sports and society until he passed away in 2016.

To this day, Muhammad Ali is still considered one of the greatest of all time.
See page for author, CC BY-SA 3.0 NL <https://creativecommons.org/licenses/by-sa/3.0/nl/deed.en>, via Wikimedia Commons
https://commons.wikimedia.org/wiki/File:Muhammad_Ali_1966.jpg

Early Life and Boxing Career

Muhammad Ali was born on January 17, 1942, in Louisville, Kentucky. He first stepped into the ring at the age of 12 and quickly realized his talent. Ali won numerous titles as an amateur boxer and went on to win the Olympic gold medal in 1960. He joined the professional ranks shortly afterward and became a heavyweight world champion at 22. Ali was the first boxer to win the heavyweight title three times.

Personality and Activism

Muhammad Ali was more than just a boxer. He was a charismatic personality with a natural gift for speaking. He was quick-witted, charming, and always ready with a good joke. But Ali was also a political and social activist, standing up for his beliefs even when it wasn't fashionable. For example, in the 1960s, he refused to be drafted into the army to fight in the Vietnam War, citing his religious beliefs and opposition. This decision cost him three years of his boxing career, but he never wavered in his views.

Ali's Philanthropy

Besides being a great athlete and activist, Muhammad Ali was a philanthropist. He was involved in numerous charitable organizations and causes, including the Make-A-Wish Foundation and the Special Olympics. He established the Muhammad Ali Center, a museum and cultural center in his hometown, Louisville, Kentucky, dedicated to promoting respect, understanding, and tolerance. Ali truly believed in giving back to his community and using his fame and influence for good.

Ali's Legacy

Muhammad Ali's legacy is of excellence, courage, and social responsibility. He was a trailblazer in the world of sports, paving the way for other African American athletes to succeed. His political and social activism inspired a generation, standing up for his beliefs even when difficult. He gave back to his community in countless ways, leaving a lasting impact on the world. Muhammad Ali's name will forever be associated with greatness, and his legacy will continue to inspire everyone for generations.

Muhammad Ali was a larger-than-life figure who left an indelible mark on the world. He was a talented athlete, a political and social activist, and a philanthropist. But most importantly, he was a great human who inspired everyone to be their best selves. Muhammad Ali's legacy and achievements will continue to be celebrated and remembered for generations, reminding people of the power of one person to make a difference.

Mike Tyson

Mike Tyson was one of the most aggressive and dominant fighters in the sport's history. He became the youngest heavyweight boxing champion at the age of 20 and held the title for three years. Tyson was known for his impressive footwork, devastating punches, and intimidating aura. He had a controversial career faced with personal struggles, but Tyson remains a popular and influential figure in the sport.

Mike Tyson became the youngest heavyweight champion at 20.
Brian Birzer http://www.brianbirzer.com, CC BY 2.0
<https://creativecommons.org/licenses/by/2.0>, via Wikimedia Commons
https://commons.wikimedia.org/wiki/File:Mike_Tyson_Portrait_lighting_corrected.jpg

Career

Mike Tyson's boxing career began in his teenage years. He made his professional debut in 1985 and quickly dominated his opponents. Tyson's style was hard-hitting and aggressive, which earned him numerous victories. He won his first twenty fights by knockouts, putting him in the spotlight as an upcoming superstar. Tyson won his first world title in 1986 by defeating Trevor Berbick and became the youngest heavyweight champion in the sport's history.

Notable Victories

Tyson's style and success in the ring continued cementing his legacy as one of the greatest boxers of all time. He was feared for his power and agility and went on to win more world titles throughout his career. Tyson's notable victories include his knockout of Larry Holmes, his victory over Michael Spinks, and his fight against Frank Bruno, where he won the WBC championship. Tyson retired from professional boxing in 2005 with 50 wins, six losses, and two no-contests. His power and dedication to the sport made him an icon and role model for boxers worldwide. Tyson's legacy in boxing is undeniable – and regarded as one of the greatest boxers in history.

Tyson's Personality

Tyson's impact extends beyond the boxing ring. His personality and charisma made him a pop culture icon. He has appeared in numerous movies, TV shows, and music videos. In addition, Tyson's memoir, "Undisputed Truth," tells his life story and gives audiences a better understanding of the man behind the gloves. Mike Tyson's legacy and achievements as a boxer have inspired many. His strength, resilience, and dedication to the sport have made him a legend. Tyson's career might have been marred with controversies, but his determination to overcome them made him a role model for boxers worldwide. He will always be remembered as one of the greatest boxers ever, and his impact on the sport of boxing will never be forgotten.

Floyd Mayweather Jr.

Floyd Mayweather Jr., known as "Money," is a retired American boxer who needs no introduction. He is considered one of the greatest boxers of all time, with unparalleled achievements in the sport. Floyd Mayweather Jr. made a name for himself with his unbeatable fighting style, an impressive record of wins, and a lavish lifestyle outside the ring. In addition, Mayweather Jr.'s talent and dedication have earned him worldwide recognition, and he is hailed by many as the best defensive boxer of all time. Let's delve into his legacy and achievements as a boxer and understand what made him the undefeated champion.

Background and Career

Mayweather Jr. was born in Grand Rapids, Michigan, on February 24, 1977. He began training at an early age, inspired by his family's boxing background. His father, uncles, and grandfather were all fighters, and they instilled discipline, hard work, and determination in him. Mayweather Jr.'s professional boxing career began in 1996 when he won his first pro-fight against Roberto Apodaca. He went on to win many more titles, including the WBC super featherweight title, WBC lightweight title, WBA (Super) light middleweight title, WBC light middleweight title, WBA (Super) welterweight title, WBC welterweight title, WBA (Super) light welterweight title, IBF welterweight title, and the WBO welterweight title.

Notable Victories

Mayweather Jr. is known for his famous bout with Manny Pacquiao in 2015, dubbed the "Fight of the Century." Mayweather Jr. won the fight via unanimous decision, retaining his undefeated record. Mayweather Jr.'s defensive fighting style sets him apart from other boxers. He has never been knocked out or knocked down, emphasizing his ability to avoid punches and maintain control in the ring. His technique has inspired many young boxers, and his dedication to training is commendable. Apart from his achievements in the ring, Mayweather Jr. is known for his lavish lifestyle. He often flaunts his wealth, fancy cars, private jets, and expensive watches. His fans love him for his flamboyant personality and confidence inside and outside the ring.

Floyd Mayweather Jr.'s legacy as a boxer will always remain unparalleled. His unbeatable record, impressive title collection, and defensive fighting style make him one of the greatest boxers ever. He has inspired many young boxers with his dedication to training and perfecting his craft. His lavish lifestyle outside the ring has made him a celebrity. Floyd Mayweather Jr.'s legacy as a boxer will continue to inspire and awe people for generations.

Other Notable Boxers

Apart from Ali and Tyson, many other legendary boxers have been during the Common Era, including Sugar Ray Leonard, Julio Cesar Chavez, Oscar De La Hoya, and Manny Pacquiao. These men brought their unique style and personality to the ring and built legacies impacting generations. They have left their mark on boxing, sports, and society, inspiring people worldwide to embrace the sport, pursue their dreams, and overcome adversities. Their achievements and contributions continue to be celebrated and studied in various ways, from books and documentaries to films and art. They have set new standards for the sport, and their legacies inspire future boxers and athletes to chase greatness.

Boxing is still one of the most loved and watched sports worldwide. Today, many talented boxers are dedicated to the sport and building their legacies. The impact of Ali, Tyson, and other notable boxers of the Common Era continues as younger fighters strive to emulate their style and success. The sport would not be the same without these great men, whose legacies will continue to inspire and entertain people worldwide.

Boxing is a timeless art, and future generations of fighters will continue learning from the achievements of the greats who came before them.

This chapter covered the origins of boxing, the transformation of the sport during the Common Era, and some of the most notable boxers from this time. From Muhammad Ali to Floyd Mayweather, Jr., these men uniquely shaped the sport and left an indelible mark on boxing, society, and the world. The legacies of these greats continue to inspire and entertain people of all ages, and their achievements will be studied, celebrated, and emulated for years to come.

Chapter 2: Getting Started with Boxing I: Rules and Fighting Styles

Do you want to get into boxing but need help figuring out where to start? Then, it's time to gear up and learn the rules and fighting styles.

Boxing is an exercise and an exhilarating sport to watch and participate in. There are a variety of fighting styles to choose from, each with unique techniques and strategies. However, before stepping into the ring, it's critical to understand the basic rules of boxing, proper fighting stances, and how to throw punches and defend yourself.

This chapter covers the general rules of boxing, the Queensberry Code of Rules for Boxing, and various fighting styles. From swarmers and counterpunchers to sluggers and out-boxers, it provides a detailed description of each type so you can discover which one suits you best. The love of boxing can be shared with friends, family, or strangers. So, let's get into the nitty-gritty of boxing and explore some basic boxing rules.

General Rules of Boxing: Everything You Need to Know

Boxing is a sport admired by millions of people around the world.

Boxing is one of the most popular sports worldwide, with millions of fans enjoying the excitement and thrill of every match. However, correctly understanding the rules and regulations is essential to enjoy the game and appreciate the art of boxing. Here are the general rules – essential to know before you start watching or participating in this sport.

Objective

The primary objective of a boxing match is to win by either knockout or points, depending on the form of the sport. A knockout victory requires knocking out the opponent so that they cannot return to the fight by the count of 10, or a referee stops the match because the boxer is in danger of serious injury or harm (technical knockout). In contrast, a victory by points is when a fighter lands more successful punches on the opponent within the duration of the match.

Scoring

Scoring in boxing is based on the number of successful punches landed throughout the match. In addition, judges evaluate and score each boxer on their ability to land punches on the opponent's body or head. The punch must land with the front part of the hand's closed glove, and only punches landed above the waist are considered. Punches below the waist are considered fouls unless the boxer's head is lowered to that level.

Fouls

Boxing has strict rules regarding a foul. Common fouls include holding, hitting below the belt, hitting the back of the head, and headbutting. Boxers are not allowed to use their elbows or other parts of their body to hit the opponent. Furthermore, boxers must not bite, spit, or intentionally cause harm to their opponent.

The Tone of Voice

A boxer must maintain a respectful tone and conduct when boxing. Disrespectful behavior like taunting an opponent or using abusive language is considered unprofessional and is potentially dangerous. Boxers must follow the referee's instructions and stop fighting when instructed. Failure to do so can lead to disqualification.

Protective Gear

Protective gear is essential for amateur and professional boxers. The most important protective equipment is a mouthguard that protects the teeth and gums from damage. Boxers are advised to wear hand wraps and gloves to protect the hands and wrists from fractures during impact. Moreover, boxing headgear protects the head and face from cuts and bruises. Boxers who compete professionally typically only wear gloves and a mouthguard, but amateur boxers usually wear more protective gear.

The Queensberry Code of Rules for Boxing: A Brief History

Boxing is a sport that has been around since the ancient Greeks, but it was in the mid-19th century that a standard set of rules was established. The Queensberry Code of Rules for Boxing was introduced in 1867, heralding a new era of boxing emphasizing safety, fair play, and sportsmanship. Let's explore the origins of the Queensberry Code, its key features, and its impact on the sport of boxing.

Origins of the Queensberry Code

Before the establishment of the Queensberry Code, boxing was a brutal and often deadly sport. Fight organizers often pitted men of vastly different sizes against each other, leading to injuries and death. The rules were minimal, and fights would continue until one fighter was incapacitated. Eventually, it led to a public outcry and calls for reform. In 1865, John Sholto Douglas, the 9th Marquess of Queensberry, wrote a letter to the Sporting Life newspaper calling for a standard set of rules governing the sport of boxing. Two years later, the Queensberry Code was published, ushering in a new era of fair play and safety in boxing.

Key Features of the Queensberry Code

The Queensberry Code established several new rules still used in boxing today. Firstly, it mandated using gloves to reduce injuries and deaths in the sport. It established the length of rounds (three minutes), the number of rounds (up to 15), and the duration of breaks between rounds (one minute). The Code introduced the concept of "down and out" – if a fighter was knocked to the ground and could not get up within 10 seconds, the fight was over. In addition, the Queensberry Code prohibited grappling, wrestling, and other forms of "foul" play.

The Impact of the Queensberry Code

The Queensberry Code had an immediate and profound impact on boxing. It made boxing safer for fighters and more palatable to audiences, increasing its popularity. The Code gave rise to a new breed of professional boxers trained in boxing rather than relying on brute strength. In addition, it established the framework for modern boxing matches, including weight classes, rankings, and championship bouts. Today, the Queensberry Code remains the basis for boxing rules in most countries worldwide.

The Queensberry Code of Rules for Boxing was a landmark moment in the sport's history. It transformed boxing from a brutal and often deadly spectacle into a sport emphasizing skill, sportsmanship, and fair play. The Code established a standard set of rules and set the stage for modern boxing as we now know it. Thanks to the vision of John Sholto Douglas, the 9th Marquess of Queensberry, boxing is a safer and more respected sport.

Different Fighting Styles

Boxing is a sport requiring precision, strength, and agility. With so many different fighting styles, each boxer brings a unique approach to the ring, from the flashy footwork of Muhammad Ali to the devastating uppercuts of Mike Tyson. The diversity of boxing styles allows for an exciting match every time. Whether a boxer prefers the defensive tactics of counterpunching or the relentless offense of swarming, the beauty of this sport lies in the creativity and adaptability of each fighter. So, who will come out on top in the ring? The answer lies in the fighters' unique combination of strategy and athleticism.

The Swarmer Style: The Art of Pressure Fighting in Boxing

Each boxing style has its unique charm. The Swarmer Style is about non-stop aggression and pressure. Swarmers are well-known for their relentless approach and constant pressure. They spend most of their time on the inside, throwing hard punches and combinations. Let's delve deeper into the Swarmer style, explore its history, and explain how it works.

Origins

The Swarmer boxing style emerged in the early 20th century and was popularized by boxers like Rocky Marciano and Joe Frazier. The style is characterized by the boxer's ability to get inside their opponent's guard and throw quick, powerful punches from close range. In addition, swarmers are known for their high stamina and intense pressure on their opponents. They apply constant and unrelenting pressure to wear their opponents down.

Basics

Swarmer boxers are usually shorter but have a powerful physique and high endurance. Their strategy is to get inside their opponent's guard and throw multiple punches quickly. They aim to keep their opponents on the back foot, pressing forward and throwing combinations. This style is excellent for boxers with strong chins and can absorb punches because they typically get hit quite often.

Attributes

One critical attribute of a Swarmer boxer is their footwork. They must be fast and agile on their feet to get inside their opponent's guard and throw punches. Swarmers are adept at slipping punches and weaving their way inside their opponent's guard. However, they need excellent reflexes and a sense of distance to land effective punches.

In Popular Culture

The Swarmer style has been significantly used by boxers like Mike Tyson, known for his relentless attacks, quick combinations, and ferocious punching power. Tyson used this style to win the heavyweight championship at the age of 20, making him the youngest heavyweight champion in history. Other notable boxers who used the Swarmer style include Joe Frazier, Roberto Duran, and Julio Cesar Chavez.

The Swarmer style is an exciting and effective way of fighting in boxing. Its style requires high endurance, excellent footwork, and relentless pressure on the opponent. Swarmers are known for their ability to get inside their opponent's guard and throw powerful punches in quick succession.

Unleashing the Strength of the Out-Boxer Boxing Style

Boxing is a combat sport requiring discipline, focus, speed, and strategy to win. One of the most compelling boxing styles is the out-boxer technique. This style emphasizes long-range punches, mobility, and footwork to outmaneuver the opponent. Here's a brief overview of the out-boxer boxing style, how it works, and why it is an excellent strategy for a boxer's arsenal.

The out-boxer style is often called the "hit and don't get hit" style of boxing. The primary goal is to maintain a safe range away from the opponent, utilizing a lot of footwork and mobility while focusing on long-range punches. This technique requires quick reflexes, accurate timing, and excellent hand-eye coordination, which is essential for any successful boxer.

A boxer must be familiar with the different punches and combinations to use the out-boxer technique effectively. The jab is a standard punch used for offense and defense. It effectively keeps opponents at a distance while setting up other punches. The cross, hook, and uppercut are punches used in the out-boxer style. These punches create angles, disrupt an opponent's balance, and create openings for counterattacks.

Footwork is an integral part of the out-boxer fighting style. Fighters must be mobile and efficient at moving in and out of range while maintaining proper balance and technique. The out-boxer footwork combines pivoting, circling, and lateral movement, allowing them to outmaneuver their opponents quickly and efficiently. Defense is significant in the out-boxer style, focusing on defense before offense. They use their footwork to circle and evade their opponents' punches and rely on their boxing stance, head movement, and combination of blocks, slips, and parries to avoid getting hit while setting up counterattacks.

One challenge of the out-boxer style is it requires exceptional stamina. Boxers must move quickly for an extended time, throw long-range punches, and maintain their accuracy, timing, and speed. They must have the patience to wait for the right moment to strike, using superior movement to create opportunities for landing decisive blows. The out-boxer style is an excellent boxing strategy, offering a unique blend of speed, accuracy, and mobility. It is an intelligent technique allowing the boxer to control the pace of the fight while keeping your opponent at a safe distance. However, mastering this style requires discipline, focus, consistent training, and developing specific skills and techniques.

Aspiring boxers can learn more about and master the out-boxer style by observing and emulating successful out-boxer fighters and working with experienced coaches who understand the nuances of this fighting style. If you aspire to become a successful boxer, consider incorporating the out-boxer style into your repertoire, and be prepared to unleash your strength and precision in the ring.

What's the Slugger Boxing Style, and Why Should You Try It?

Boxing gives you a full-body workout while honing your coordination and overall athleticism. However, with so many different boxing styles, finding the one that suits you best might take a lot of work - enter the Slugger Boxing Style. This boxing form combines power and aggression, so if you like getting up close and personal, this could be the perfect boxing style for you. But first, let's dive into what makes the Slugger Boxing Style so unique.

Heavy on Power

The Slugger Boxing Style is known to be heavy on power and strong blows. It means slugging is about delivering hard punches and dealing with heavy blows instead of relying on quick movements and agility like other boxing styles. The Slugger Boxing Style is perfect for those with a natural aptitude for strength and durable power.

Focused on Close-Range Combat

Another critical element of this boxing style is its focus on close-range combat. You must be comfortable in the pocket, throwing and taking punches in tight quarter circumstances to be successful in slugging. So, if you like to get in and fight dirty, the Slugger Boxing Style might be for you.

Suitable for Taller Boxers

Finding a boxing style that suits you can be challenging if you are over six feet tall. Many boxing techniques rely on agility and speed, which can be tougher to execute for taller boxers. However, the Slugger Boxing Style is perfect for a taller fighter because it emphasizes strength and power, which aligns well with boxers with a more extended reach.

Requires Proper Defense

While slugging emphasizes offense and hard-hitting blows, developing solid defense skills is crucial. Since you are constantly in your pocket, you must protect yourself from incoming punches from your opponent. Without proper defense, you open yourself up to body blows, reducing stamina, affecting your breathing, and weakening your guard. Therefore, practice your defense techniques and continuously improve them to protect yourself from vigorous attacks.

Promotes Discipline and Focus

Every boxing style requires hard work and dedication. Slugger Boxing is no exception, as it demands a lot of practice and focus, but the payoff is immense. By focusing on moves and techniques that lean into body strength and power, slugging provides discipline translating into other aspects of life. Regular practice and persistence will teach you to stay focused and overcome obstacles inside and outside the ring.

The Slugger Boxing Style is a unique boxing style that could be the perfect fit for anyone who wants to emphasize their physical power and close combat skills. This boxing technique provides a dynamic yet challenging physical way of improving your agility skills, strength, and endurance. The Slugger Boxing Style demands dedication and hard work, but the physical benefits and discipline are immense. If you're considering exploring different boxing styles, the Slugger Boxing Style is an excellent option to enhance your overall training.

Unleashing the Counterpunch: Why This Boxing Style Is Worth Learning

One technique in boxing that can give you an edge over your opponent is the counterpunch. This boxing style uses your opponent's aggressive moves and turns them into opportunities for an effective counterattack. While mastering a boxing style takes time and effort, this style is worth learning; this section explores why.

The Element of Surprise

Counterpunching is taking advantage of your opponent's expectations. One moment, they think they have the upper hand. The next, they're stunned by the effectiveness of your counterpunch. It puts you in control and can shake your opponent's confidence, making them hesitant to attack again.

The Importance of Defense

As any boxer knows, defense is as critical as offense. In counterpunching, defense is front and center. You'll focus on slipping, weaving, and blocking your opponent's attacks to create openings you can exploit with a counterpunch.

Strategic Thinking

Counterpunching requires a lot of strategy and timing. You must read your opponent's moves, anticipate their attacks, and know when to strike to maximize your counterpunch's effectiveness. This skill improves your boxing and helps you become a more strategic thinker.

Versatility

One of the most significant benefits of mastering counterpunching is its versatility. This technique can be used against various opponents, from aggressive brawlers to more calculated boxers, making it a valuable skill in your back pocket. The key is to practice, hone your skills, and stay sharp to gain an edge in the ring.

Building Confidence

Last, learning counterpunching can do wonders for your confidence in the ring. As you become more familiar with the technique, you develop better control during fights, leading to bold and confident moves, ultimately leading to better performance and victories. The confidence level of mastering this technique is hard to overstate and well worth the effort.

Counterpunching is a challenging technique to learn, but the benefits are numerous. From keeping your opponent guessing and improving your defense to building strategic thinking, versatility, and confidence, it's no wonder many boxers consider it an essential tool in their arsenal. So, consider adding this technique to your repertoire the next time you train and watch as your boxing skills and confidence grow.

Mixed Martial Arts (MMA)

Mixed Martial Arts (MMA) is a blend of various martial arts styles that focuses on striking and grappling techniques. While MMA fighters predominantly use elbows, knees, and kicks to score points or knock out their opponents, boxing is an essential aspect of the sport. Boxing-style striking highlights the importance of precise footwork, head movement, and powerful punches. Let's explore the significance of boxing in MMA and discover how MMA fighters use it to dominate their opponents in the cage.

Mixed martial arts is a blend of different styles of fighting.

Footwork and Head Movement

Boxing is all about footwork and head movement; the same applies to MMA. An MMA fighter must avoid takedowns and strikes while moving around the cage. Proper footwork allows the fighter to get in and out of range, maintain the appropriate distance, and adjust his striking angles in real-time. The head movement involves the defender moving his head to avoid a strike while simultaneously throwing a counterpunch. This technique is essential for boxers and can be integrated into MMA.

Judging Punches and Combinations

Boxing entails judging the punches thrown by the opponent and anticipating which one is coming next. Reading the opponent is incredibly important, whether via facial expressions, body language, or how he moves. A boxer must learn to throw combinations to set up his opponent and score a knockout punch. MMA fighters utilize these techniques to anticipate their opponent's moves and launch an effective counterattack.

Power Punches and Defense

A power punch is a punch with knockout power or the ability to inflict significant damage to the opponent. Power punches can be thrown from different angles and aim to put the rival down or create an opening for a follow-up strike. MMA fighters use power punches and incorporate them into ground-and-pound techniques when they take an opponent down. Similarly, boxing-style defense is an integral part of MMA. Fighters use shoulder rolls, parrying, and slipping to avoid shots and counterattacks as their opponents expose themselves.

Footwork and Cage Control

Boxing footwork emphasizes maintaining control over the ring, creating angles, and positioning for an attack or defense. In MMA, the fighter must use cage control, meaning they must stay off the cage against a wrestler or BJJ (Brazilian Jiu-Jitsu) fighter while positioning themselves to throw effective strikes. Effective footwork and cage control can make all the difference between losing and winning a match.

Conditioning and Fight IQ

Boxing in MMA requires significant conditioning, mental preparation, and fighting IQ. Fighters must be conditioned to throw punches at high intensity for several rounds while having the endurance to grapple in the later rounds. Fight IQ involves a high combat awareness level enabling a fighter to adapt to the pace of a match, stay composed, and execute strategies based on the opponent's skills. To be a top-tier MMA boxer with a fight IQ, you must box regularly, focus on conditioning, study your opponent, and learn new techniques.

Whether it's footwork, head movement, power punches, defense, or even fight IQ, boxing can give MMA fighters the advantage to dominate and win their battles. Furthermore, properly learning and utilizing these techniques significantly improves fighters' chances of winning a match. Therefore, aspiring MMA fighters should incorporate boxing into their training regimen to elevate their game, increase their chances of succeeding, and ultimately become champions.

Boxing is a sport not for the faint of heart. It aims to knock out or score more points than your opponent by landing punches. However, many rules and regulations must be followed to ensure a fair fight. No boxer would deliberately choose to be penalized for fouls.

The Queensberry Code of Rules for Boxing is the standard for all boxing matches. Beyond the rules are different fighting styles boxers adopt. Some are swarmers - always on the offensive, while others are out-boxers who prefer to fight from a distance. Some sluggers go for the knockout punch, and counterpunchers wait to strike. Due to the rise of Mixed Martial Arts (MMA), boxing has taken on a new dimension. With so many styles and rules, boxing will always keep you on your toes.

Chapter 3: Getting Started with Boxing II: Gear and Physical Conditioning

Are you ready to start your boxing journey? If you're serious about becoming a boxer, you must invest in high-quality gear and equipment. From gloves and clothing to hand wraps and fitness equipment, your gear is pivotal in ensuring you stay safe and perform your best. Whether you're looking for breathable fabrics or padding, choosing the right apparel can significantly affect your comfort and performance. Starting with the right gear and equipment is essential if you're ready to train like a professional boxer.

This chapter discusses various boxing apparel and equipment types, including hand wraps and gloves. It looks at fitness techniques to condition your body for the match. The chapter concludes with expert boxers' tips on physical training. Remember, the best boxing gear and fitness techniques will only be effective if you have the proper diet. By the end of this chapter, you should understand the intricacies of boxing better.

The Ultimate Guide to Boxing Gear, Clothing, and Equipment

If you're passionate about boxing, you know that the right gear can make all the difference to your training and performance. However, choosing your equipment and clothing can be overwhelming with so many options available. This section explores everything you need for a successful and safe boxing routine, from gloves to mouthguards and apparel to equipment.

Gloves

6. Boxing gloves.
https://www.pexels.com/photo/boxing-gloves-and-mitts-over-the-grass-5836652/

A good pair of gloves is essential to any boxer. Gloves come in a range of weights, typically from 8 to 20 ounces. The correct weight depends on your weight and skill level. If you're a beginner, starting with a lighter glove is better. Pay attention to the fit and closure, lace-up, or Velcro when choosing gloves. Leather gloves are more durable, but hybrid gloves with nylon and synthetic leather are lighter.

Hand Wraps

7. Hand wraps protect your hands, wrists, and knuckles.
https://www.pexels.com/photo/blurred-sportswoman-demonstrating-technique-of-hand-bandaging-7991696/

Hand wraps are as essential as gloves. They protect your hands, wrists, and knuckles from injury. Wraps come in various lengths, but a 180-inch wrap is the most common. Wrapping your hands helps maintain a good grip on your gloves. The basic technique is to start by covering your wrist, knuckles, and fingers.

Mouthguards

8. Mouthguards help protect your teeth.
https://www.pexels.com/photo/smiling-man-wearing-mouth-guard-and-boxing-gloves-7289912/

Protecting your teeth is paramount in boxing. A mouthguard is a cheap and effective gear that can save you from oral and, in severe cases, brain injury. Mouthguards come in two basic types and can be customized to fit your teeth comfortably. It must be thick enough to absorb the impact of a punch.

Apparel

Proper clothing is not only essential for appearance but also critical for comfort and safety. Boxing shorts are typically loose-fitting and reach mid-thigh for maximum mobility. A good training shoe supporting your ankles is an essential piece of equipment. Last, wear a cotton shirt or vest with a sports bra (for females) for comfort.

Boxing Equipment

Last but not least is the boxing equipment. Various equipment, including speed, heavy, and double-end bags, are available. Always ensure the kit fits your physical ability. You'll get the best results from your training when you practice with the right equipment.

The Art and Science of Wrapping Your Hands for Boxing

If you're serious about boxing, you know the importance of protecting your hands during training and competitions. Proper hand wrapping provides valuable support and protection for your wrists, knuckles, and fingers. It improves your punching power and reduces the risk of injury. This section discusses the art and science of wrapping your hands for boxing.

Choose the Right Type of Hand Wraps

Various hand wraps are available on the market, from standard cotton wraps to gel wraps with added cushioning. The wrap you choose depends on your preference and needs. Cotton wraps are the most common and affordable option. However, a gel wrap could be more suitable if you require extra padding.

Prepare Your Wraps Properly

Before you start wrapping, ensure your wraps are clean and dry. Any moisture or sweat can cause irritation and discomfort during training or competition. Also, roll the wraps up tightly and store them in a sealable bag to keep them from getting tangled and to maintain their elasticity. If you're using a gel wrap, shake it before applying.

Wrapping Technique

There is no one-size-fits-all technique for wrapping your hands. There are many methods, but it's up to you to find what works best for your hand size and shape. Here's a general guide for the most common technique:

1. Start with the loop around your thumb
2. Wrap your wrist several times, creating a base for your knuckles
3. Wrap your knuckles several times, crossing the wraps over the back of your hand
4. Cover the thumb and continue wrapping down to your wrist, securing the wrap with Velcro or tape

Common Mistakes to Avoid

A few common mistakes people make when wrapping their hands can reduce the wrap's effectiveness or cause discomfort and injury. These include the following:

1. Wrapping too tightly and restricting blood flow and movement
2. Not covering the thumb, thus leaving it vulnerable
3. Covering over the knuckles too loosely or too tightly, making them weak or reducing mobility

Maintaining Your Wraps

After your training or competition, remove your wraps gently and thoroughly clean and air-dry them. Sweat and bacteria can build up, causing odor and irritation. Also, replace your wraps immediately if they have lost elasticity or show wear and tear. A loose wrap won't provide your hands with the necessary protection and support.

Hand wrapping might seem like a minor detail, but it can significantly affect your boxing performance and safety. Therefore, it's essential to choose the right wrap, prepare them properly, and use proper wrapping techniques to ensure maximum support, comfort, and protection. In addition, remember to avoid common mistakes and maintain your wraps to prolong their lifespan and effectiveness. By following these tips, you can ensure your hands are protected and empowered to deliver knockout punches in the ring.

Best Clothing and Gloves for Boxing

Whether you're new to boxing or have been practicing for a while, having the proper clothing and gloves is critical in enhancing performance and protecting yourself from injury. With endless options, figuring out the best investment items can be challenging. This section delves into the best clothing and gloves for boxing.

Boxing Gloves

Boxing gloves are the most critical gear in the sport. They protect your hands and wrists from injury while delivering powerful punches. The glove you choose should be based on your goals and experience level. Ideally, beginners should choose a lighter pair of gloves ranging between 10-14 ounces, whereas professionals can go for heavier gloves of 16-20 ounces. EverLast, Cleto Reyes, Winning, and Rival manufacture the best gloves.

Boxing Shoes

Boxing shoes can help you perform better.
https://unsplash.com/photos/qPhXapAS2Ss?utm_source=unsplash&utm_medium=referral&utm_content=creditShareLink

Boxing shoes should be lightweight, supportive, and stable when you move around the ring. Look for shoes with a rubber sole to help you pivot better and a high ankle providing ample support and preventing your ankles from rolling. Adidas, Title, and Ringside are top brands to check out when shopping for boxing shoes.

Boxing Shorts

Boxing shorts don't have to be expensive, but they should be comfortable and allow free movement. Avoid cotton shorts as they absorb too much sweat and become heavy. Instead, opt for nylon or polyester with split side seams to enhance flexibility. Some recommended top brands include RDX, Venum, and Hayabusa.

Boxing Headgear

If you want to spar, you must wear protective headgear. Headgear offers extra protection, reducing the risk of cuts and brain injuries. Your headgear should fit snugly and have adequate padding to absorb impacts. Some popular brands known for producing top-quality headgear include Title, Ringside, and Winning.

Boxing gear is an essential investment to improve your boxing skills. The right gear enhances your performance and keeps you safe from injury. Boxing gloves, shoes, shorts, hand wraps, and headgear are the most critical items in your gear bag. Consider investing in high-quality gear from trusted brands, and you'll take one step closer to becoming a pro.

Fitness for Boxers: Train Your Body and Mind to Become a Champion

Boxing is one of the most popular sports in the world and a great way to stay fit and healthy. Much effort and dedication go into becoming a successful boxer. It's not only about hitting hard but about technique, speed, agility, and endurance. This section discusses all things related to fitness for boxers.

Can Anyone Start Training as a Boxer?

The answer is a big YES. Anyone passionate about boxing and dedication can start learning and training as a boxer. No matter your age or body type, boxing is for everyone. However, it's crucial to know that boxing is an intense sport requiring focus and discipline. So, if you are willing to put in the hard work and sweat, there's no reason you can't become a great boxer.

Training Your Body to Box

Boxing is an intense sport demanding a lot from your body, so proper preparation is essential. Cardiovascular exercises are a fundamental aspect of boxing, so include running, jumping rope, and cycling in your workout routine. In addition, strength training exercises like push-ups, pull-ups, and squats are a must for building strong arms, legs, and core.

Diet and Its Role in Boxing

A healthy and balanced diet is equally vital for boxers to perform at their best. Fighters need a lot of energy to keep up with rigorous training and matches. Eating a protein-rich diet, carbohydrates, and healthy fats is best. Include chicken, fish, whole grains, vegetables, and fruit. Staying hydrated throughout the day is crucial, as dehydration can affect your performance negatively.

Mental Health and Boxing

Boxing requires immense focus and mental strength. A boxer's mental state will affect their performance, so working on your mental health is essential. Practice meditation, yoga, or visualization to stay calm and focused during your fights. Furthermore, setting achievable goals and celebrating your achievements is important.

General Strength Training

Strength training is no longer just for bodybuilders or weightlifters. It has become an indispensable part of any fitness routine, and everyone, regardless of age or gender, can benefit. As experts in strength training, boxers have many valuable insights to share. Their training regimes are about improving their boxing abilities and overall strength and conditioning. This section covers some of the best-talented boxers' general strength training tips.

Don't Skip the Warm-Up

Before an intense workout, it is essential to do a proper warm-up. Boxers recommend starting with light aerobic exercises to get your blood flowing. Some of their favorite warm-up exercises include jumping jacks, jogging, skipping rope, and shadowboxing. These exercises help to increase the heart rate, warm up the muscles, and reduce the risk of injury.

Focus on Compound Exercises

The best way to build overall strength is by focusing on compound exercises. These exercises involve multiple muscle groups simultaneously. Examples of compound exercises include squats, lunges, deadlifts, bench presses, and pull-ups. These movements help develop strength and stability, benefiting your boxing techniques and overall physical health.

Incorporate Plyometric Exercises

Plyometric exercises involve jumping and explosive movements to develop explosive power. Boxers often include plyometric exercises to improve speed, agility, and coordination. Plyometric exercises include box jumps, burpees, jump squats, clap push-ups, and more.

Take Rest Days

It's essential to avoid overtraining, and expert boxers recommend rest days between workouts to allow the muscle fibers to regenerate and repair. Rest is as important as exercise for building strength, so schedule enough rest time into your routine. Aim for two to three days of rest a week. Focus on strength training exercises for the remaining days.

Be Consistent

Consistency is the key to achieving strength training goals. It's not about working out every day for a week and giving up the next. Instead, it's about maintaining and sticking to a consistent routine for long-term results. The boxers recommend aiming for at least three to four strength training sessions a week and gradually increasing the weights over time.

Incorporating strength training into your fitness routines helps you build stronger muscles, increases endurance, and improves your overall physical health. In strength training, listening to and learning from experts like boxers can help you create a more effective workout routine. Remember to incorporate warm-up exercises, focus on compound exercises, include plyometric exercises, take rest days, and consistently train. By following these tips, you can achieve your strength training goals and improve your overall health.

Core Exercises to Improve Punching Power

Whether you are a professional boxer or enjoy practicing martial arts, a solid core is essential for delivering powerful punches. Core strength refers to the abdominals, back, and hip muscles that all work together to stabilize your body and transfer force from the ground up through your fists. This section explores five practical core exercises to help improve your punching power, taking your game to the next level.

Plank

Planks are excellent for building core strength by engaging your entire midsection, including abs, back, and hips. The basic plank involves holding a push-up position for as long as possible, keeping your body straight and parallel to the ground. To add an extra challenge, perform plank variations, like side planks, leg lifts, or walking planks. Incorporating planks into your workout routine, you develop excellent stability and control, allowing you to throw more powerful punches with less effort.

Russian Twist

The Russian Twist is an excellent exercise to target your obliques, the muscles on the sides of your waist. To perform this exercise:

1. Sit on the ground with your feet flat on the floor and your knees bent.

2. Hold a weight or medicine ball with both hands and twist your torso to the right, touching the weight to the ground.

3. Turn to the left and repeat the movement. This exercise develops rotational power in your torso, which is essential for generating force in your punches.

Russian twist.

Dead Bug

The Dead Bug exercise targets your lower abs and helps improve your core muscle stability. To perform this exercise:

1. Lie on your back with your arms and legs extended toward the ceiling.

2. Lower your right arm and left leg until they hover just above the ground, then return to the starting position and repeat on the opposite side.

3. Keep your lower back pressed into the ground to prevent arching and maintain proper form as you perform this exercise.

Dead bug.

Medicine Ball Slam

Medicine ball slams are a fantastic way to develop explosive power in your punches by training your body to transfer force quickly. To perform this exercise, stand with your feet shoulder-width apart and hold a medicine ball overhead. Slam the ball onto the ground as hard as possible, then catch it on the rebound and repeat. This exercise will help you improve your speed and power, so you can deliver lightning-fast punches that pack a punch.

Medicine ball slam.

Bicycle Crunches

Bicycle crunches are a classic core exercise targeting your abs and obliques, developing rotational power in your torso. To perform this exercise:

1. Lie on your back with your hands behind your head and your knees bent.
2. Lift your shoulder blades off the ground and bring your right elbow toward your left knee while extending your right leg straight.
3. Switch sides and repeat.

Performing many reps of bicycle crunches develops endurance and core strength, which are essential for boxing.

Bicycle crunches.

Improving your punching power requires a combination of training and technique, but strengthening your core through targeted exercises makes a substantial difference. Incorporate these five core exercises into your workout routine, and you'll see noticeable improvements in your stability, power, and speed. Remember to focus on proper form and gradually increase the exercises' intensity over time for the best results. You will take your punching power to the next level and dominate in the ring with dedication and consistency.

Interval Training and Other Options to Improve as a Boxer

Are you a boxer looking for ways to improve your skills? Or maybe you're just starting and want to know how to improve? Whatever your situation, this section introduces you to interval training and other options to improve as a boxer. These tips will refine your skills, build endurance, and achieve your goals in the ring.

Interval Training

Interval training is great for building endurance and increasing fitness levels. This training involves alternating periods of intense exercise with rest periods. For example, you could sprint for 30 seconds and then rest for 30 seconds. This cycle could be repeated for a set time or a certain number of reps. Interval training is practical because it pushes your body to work harder, burning more calories and building stamina. Incorporate interval training into your workout routine for optimal benefits.

Shadow Boxing

Shadowboxing is another effective way to improve as a boxer. This training technique involves practicing your moves without an opponent. It can be done anywhere and is a great way to work on footwork, punches, and combinations. Focus on perfecting your form and technique and speed up your movements as you become more comfortable. Shadowboxing can be a warm-up or a standalone exercise to improve your skills.

Sparring

Sparring is an essential component of boxing training. It allows you to practice your moves in a realistic setting and to learn from your mistakes. Sparring is done with a partner or a coach and is excellent for improving reaction time and agility. Wear proper safety gear and start slowly to avoid injury. Then, as you become more experienced, gradually increase your sparring session's intensity.

Cardiovascular Conditioning

Cardiovascular conditioning is crucial for any athlete, especially boxers. It improves endurance and increases the high work rate during fights. Incorporate cardiovascular training into your routine by running, swimming, cycling, or using a cardio machine at the gym. Aim for at least 30 minutes of cardiovascular exercise daily or longer if you're preparing for a fight.

Invest in quality gloves, hand wraps, and a mouthguard to protect you from injury and confidence in the ring. Once you have your gear, it's time to focus on your physical conditioning. Boxing requires strength, endurance, and agility, so incorporate cardio, strength training, and flexibility exercises into your routine. Remember, working on your footwork and balance is imperative. With the right gear and physical preparation, you'll be ready to step into the ring and unleash your inner boxer.

Chapter 4: Stances, Guards, and Footwork

Boxing is an incredible sport requiring physical strength, mental agility, and quick reflexes. One of the most important aspects of boxing is your stance, which determines the effectiveness of your movements and punches. A strong and stable stance is critical to getting the upper hand in any match. Guards are equally essential to protect yourself from incoming punches and to set up offensive strikes. But don't forget the footwork. Proper footwork allows you to move around the ring confidently and dodge incoming blows.

These components together make for an exciting and dynamic fight, and mastering these skills can bring you one step closer to becoming a champion. This chapter provides essential stances, guards, and footwork techniques to help you get started. Training your body, mind, and spirit is necessary to becoming a well-rounded boxer. Take the tips from the experts mentioned in this chapter to heart, and you will be well on your way to improving your skills and taking your boxing game to the next level.

Getting in Position: Understanding Different Boxing Stances

One of the first things you learn when training for boxing is the importance of your stance. How you position your feet, hands, and body makes all the difference to the success of your punches and the effectiveness of your defense. This section tackles the basics of the most common boxing stances and gives tips on switching between them seamlessly.

The Orthodox Stance

The orthodox stance is considered the normal boxing stance.

The orthodox stance is the most common in boxing. It's so well known that it's often called the "normal" stance. In a traditional stance, your left side faces forward, and your left foot is ahead of your right. Your left hand is held to protect your face, while your right hand is held close to your chin to set up powerful punches. This stance provides a good combination of offense and defense, so many beginner boxers start here. Remember, always keep your left elbow tucked close to your body in an orthodox stance.

The Southpaw Stance

The Southpaw stance is less common in boxing.

The Southpaw stance is less common but is still essential in boxing. In this stance, your right side faces forward, and your right foot is ahead of your left. Your left hand is held close to your face while your right hand is extended to deliver jabs and hooks. Southpaws can be challenging to fight because their stance is unfamiliar to most boxers, and their punches come from unexpected angles. This stance requires more skill and practice to master. However, once you're comfortable, the Southpaw stance can be great for surprising your opponents.

Switching Stances

The ability to switch stances quickly is necessary for boxers.

Boxers must have the ability to switch stances quickly and effectively. This skill can be a powerful weapon when fighting against opponents more comfortable fighting from a particular stance. To switch stances, step forward or backward with your back foot, pivot your front foot, and rotate your hips. Keep your guard up throughout the transition to protect yourself from counterpunches. Practice switching stances regularly to ensure you are comfortable and confident with the orthodox and southpaw stances.

Stance Adjustments

A boxer's stance must be adjusted depending on the situation. For example, if you're fighting a taller opponent, lowering your stance to get under their punches and delivering powerful shots to their body is beneficial. Alternatively, raising your stance is more effective for keeping them at a distance if you're fighting a shorter opponent. Therefore, pay attention to your opponent's stance and adjust yours to gain the upper hand.

Benefits of Proper Stance

A proper boxing stance can deliver powerful, precise punches while keeping you safe from your opponent's strikes. The correct posture improves your balance and footwork, allowing you to move quickly and efficiently in the ring. When you're in the right position, you have a much more effective defense and can set up powerful combinations to knock out even the toughest opponents.

Your stance is the foundation of your boxing technique, and it's essential to master it early in your training. By understanding the different stances, practicing switching between them, and adjusting for various situations, you'll be well on your way to becoming a formidable fighter. Remember, a proper boxing stance isn't just about looking good in the ring; it's about delivering powerful punches while avoiding your opponent's strikes. With time, practice, and dedication, you can become a skilled boxer with an impressive command of the different stances. So, get in position and let those punches fly!

Getting Defensive: Guards and Blocking Techniques

In most sports, defense is as important as offense. After all, even the best teams can't win if they don't stop the opposition. It is especially true in combat sports like boxing and martial arts, where the ability to defend is essential. One of the most critical aspects of defense is using guards and blocking techniques. This section explores three standard methods; the high guard, the low guard, and slip and roll. You'll better understand how to defend yourself against your opponents.

The High Guard

The high guard can be beneficial to defend your face.

The first technique is the high guard. It is one of the most common techniques in combat sports, particularly boxing. Raise both hands before your face to do a high guard. Your palms should face inward, and your fingers tightly clenched. Your elbows should be close to your rib cage to protect your body. With a high guard, you can deflect many punches, especially those aimed at your head. The downside of a high guard is it can be challenging to counterpunch effectively, so it's best used in a defensive position.

The Low Guard

The low guard can be beneficial when defending your body.

Another technique is the low guard. This technique is beneficial when you're defending your body. Lower your hands and bring them closer to your body for a low guard. Your palms should face outward, and your fingers relaxed. Bend your knees slightly to make it harder for your opponent to land a punch to your stomach. With a low guard, you can better defend your body, but you are more vulnerable to punches aimed at your head, so keeping your head moving is essential.

Slip and Roll

The slip-and-roll technique will leave your opponent vulnerable.
Alain Delmas (France), CC BY-SA 3.0 <http://creativecommons.org/licenses/by-sa/3.0/>, via
Wikimedia Commons: https://commons.wikimedia.org/wiki/File:Slip1.jpg

Last is the slip-and-roll technique. This technique involves moving your body out of your opponent's punches. Move your head to one side and pivot on your front foot to make a slip; it causes your opponent's punch to miss you completely. To do a roll, you must lean to one side, bend your knees, and pivot on your back foot. Again, this will cause your opponent's punch to graze past you. Slip and roll are fantastic techniques for a counterpunch, as they leave your opponent vulnerable and off balance.

These three standard guards and blocking techniques are for defending yourself in combat sports. Each method has strengths and weaknesses, so it's essential to practice and use them strategically, depending on the situation. With enough practice, you will anticipate your opponent's moves and defend yourself effectively. Remember, defense is as important as offense, and the best defense is a good offense. So, keep practicing, keep learning, and you'll be an unbeatable opponent in no time.

Mastering Footwork Techniques: Tips and Drills

Boxing is a great physical workout and art form. One of the most critical aspects of this art form is footwork. Footwork is essential since it provides balance and power to a boxer's strikes, allowing them to move around the ring with speed and agility. This section delves into the essential footwork techniques every fighter should know. Included are tips and tricks to improve your footwork immediately. Last, here are some drills to help you master these techniques.

Step and Slide

This technique can help you efficiently move away from your opponent.

Footwork is about positioning yourself correctly to throw punches while quickly and efficiently moving out of harm's way. One of the most basic footwork techniques is the "step and slide." This technique involves stepping with your lead foot toward your opponent, sliding your back foot forward, and placing it next to your lead foot. This moves your body forward with your lead foot while maintaining balance. Not stepping too far or close to your opponent is important, or you'll risk losing balance or opening up to counterpunches.

Pivot

Pivots can help you control the direction of your body.

This technique can control the direction of your body while throwing a punch or moving around the ring. A pivot is a movement of the front foot, turning it to the side so that your body turns while maintaining balance. When pivoting, it's vital to keep your back foot anchored or to move it only slightly so you don't lose balance. Pivoting quickly and efficiently improves your maneuverability, allowing you to avoid your opponent's punches or get closer to throwing a punch.

Lateral Movement

Lateral movement is another critical aspect of footwork in boxing. A great way to practice lateral movement is a ladder drill. A ladder drill is placing a ladder flat on the ground and moving up and down it, keeping your feet inside each rung. This drill improves quickness and agility, which are essential when evading punches or moving around the ring.

Footwork Drills

In addition to practicing moving forward, backward, and laterally, specific footwork drills will improve your footwork. One drill is the Slalom Drill - set up cones in a zigzag formation and practice shuffling through them from side to side. Another drill is the Jump Rope Drill - jump over a rope while keeping your feet together, alternating between jumping forward and backward. Also, the Balance Pad Drill - stand on a balance pad and practice different footwork techniques while maintaining balance.

Incorporating speed and double-end bags into your training routine improves footwork. These bags simulate an opponent's movements, and by hitting them, you practice footwork techniques improving your reaction time. Footwork is essential in boxing because it provides balance and power to your strikes, allowing you to move around the ring with speed and agility. By incorporating these drills and techniques into your training routine, you'll master your footwork skills in no time.

Mastering footwork techniques is crucial to be successful in boxing. The proper footwork can help you avoid punches, move in and out of range, and deliver powerful strikes. Using these methods and incorporating drills into your training routine improves your footwork skills to become a more effective boxer. Remember, footwork is the foundation of boxing, so practice often and refine your skills.

Knockout Tips from Boxing Experts

Whether you're a beginner or a seasoned pro, boxing is an intense and rewarding workout. However, you must know more than just the basics to truly excel at this popular martial art. Below is a compilation of some of the best tips from boxing experts to improve your skills and reach your full potential in the ring. From staying balanced to developing mental toughness, you are covered.

Staying Balanced: Maintaining balance is crucial to throwing powerful punches and evading your opponent's attacks. Boxing experts recommend keeping your feet shoulder-width apart and slightly angled, with your weight evenly distributed. In addition, slightly bending your knees and engaging your core improves balance and mobility in the ring.

Maintaining Focus: Boxing requires intense concentration and focus, as even the slightest distraction can cost you the fight. Experts suggest practicing mindfulness and visualization techniques to help you stay focused and present in the moment. Additionally, practicing proper breathing techniques keeps your mind and body calm under pressure, which is essential for success in the ring.

Reacting Quickly: In boxing, speed is everything. One of the best ways to improve your reaction time is by training with a speed bag, a small punching bag that rebounds quickly after each punch. You will develop hand-eye coordination and reaction time by hitting it consistently and promptly.

Using Your Opponent's Movement: The best boxers know how to use their opponent's movements to their advantage. For instance, if your opponent moves to your right, you can pivot on your left foot and throw a powerful left hook. You can gain an edge in the ring by studying your opponent's style and reacting appropriately.

Blending Stances and Guards: While most boxers have a traditional stance, boxing experts suggest blending different stances and guards to keep your opponent guessing. For instance, switch between a square stance, the classic boxing stance, and a staggered stance, giving you more power and versatility in your punches. Changing your guard protects different areas of your body and throws your opponent off their game.

Developing Strength, Power, and Agility: Boxing is a physical sport and requires strength, power, and agility to succeed. To develop these skills, boxing experts suggest doing exercises like squats, burpees, and pushups. Additionally, they recommend running sprints or using an elliptical machine to improve endurance in the ring.

Working On Hand-Eye Coordination: Hand-eye coordination is a crucial skill for any boxer and can be improved through practice. To sharpen your technique, boxing experts suggest throwing drills with medicine balls or shadowboxing in front of a mirror. Additionally, they recommend working on hand-eye coordination by playing sports like tennis or basketball.

Practicing Mental Toughness: Boxing is a mental game as much as a physical one. To achieve success in the ring, boxing experts suggest developing your mental toughness by visualizing yourself winning, setting achievable goals, and pushing yourself to be your best. Additionally, they recommend visualizing every punch you throw and establishing a positive mindset before each fight.

Improving Speed and Cardiovascular Endurance: You must throw fast, powerful punches and move quickly to reach your maximum potential in the ring. To improve your speed and cardiovascular endurance, boxing experts suggest interval training or short-distance running sprints. Additionally, they recommend focusing on exercises targeting the legs to increase your overall power and mobility in the ring.

Taking Care Of Your Body: Boxing is a physically demanding sport, and taking care of your body after each fight is essential. Boxing experts recommend gently stretching your muscles, getting plenty of sleep, eating healthy meals, and cooling down with light exercise or yoga. Additionally, they suggest using ice packs on sore areas and drinking plenty of water to stay hydrated.

Training with a Partner or Instructor: Boxing is a complex sport, so it's essential to have someone to guide and help you develop your technique. To ensure you get the most out of training, boxing experts suggest working with an experienced partner or instructor. You will receive feedback on your technique and practice different combinations in a safe environment.

Analyzing Your Fights and Performance: You must know your weaknesses and strengths to become a better boxer. After each fight, boxing experts suggest watching footage of the match and analyzing your performance. You will identify areas needing improvement and develop strategies for future conflicts. Additionally, they recommend getting feedback from coaches or instructors on your technique so you can make the necessary adjustments.

Properly Wrapping Your Hands: Correctly wrapping your hands is an essential skill for any boxer and helps prevent injury in the ring. To wrap your hands properly, boxing experts suggest placing four-to-six inches of gauze around each hand. Then, add a layer of athletic tape above that. Finally, secure the ends with adhesive tape so the wrap is snug and secure.

Eating a Balanced Diet and Staying Hydrated: Eating a balanced diet and staying hydrated is critical to performing at your best in the ring. To fuel your training, boxing experts suggest eating plenty of lean proteins, whole grains, and fruits and vegetables. Additionally, they recommend drinking plenty of water throughout the day to keep your body hydrated and functioning optimally.

Getting Enough Rest: Rest and recovery are essential for any athlete, especially boxers. To ensure you get enough rest, boxing experts recommend aiming for eight hours of sleep each night. They suggest short breaks throughout the day to avoid fatigue and burnout.

Taking Time to Recover after Training Sessions: Boxing is a physically demanding sport, and giving your body time for proper recovery after each training session is essential. To help speed up the recovery process, boxing experts suggest taking an ice bath after each workout and using compression garments to reduce swelling and soreness. Additionally, they recommend taking a few days off each week to give your body an extra chance to rest and recover.

Staying Positive: A positive attitude can make all the difference in success in the ring. To stay motivated and focused on training, boxing experts suggest setting realistic goals and celebrating each milestone. Additionally, they recommend surrounding yourself with positive people who support and encourage you in your journey.

Learning from The Best: Learning from the best is essential to become a better boxer. Boxing experts suggest watching footage of world-class fighters and studying their techniques. Additionally, they recommend reading books and articles written by experienced boxers to gain insight into the sport's strategies and tactics.

Practicing Visualization Techniques: Mental strength is as important as physical strength in boxing. To help enhance your mental game, boxing experts suggest practicing visualization techniques. For instance, picture yourself in a fight and visualize the moves you must make to succeed. Additionally, they recommend setting aside time each day to practice visualization techniques and build mental toughness.

Finishing Strong: To finish strong in a fight, boxing experts suggest saving energy for the final rounds. They suggest staying focused on your goals and visualizing success to stay motivated until the end. Additionally, they recommend taking deep breaths to help you remain calm and energized in the final moments of a match.

Feet Shoulder-Width Apart: To improve your performance, start by focusing on the position of your feet. Ensure they are shoulder-width apart. Next, stand straight and hold your hands near your head. This stance lets you move around the ring quickly, maintain balance, and deliver powerful punches.

Move Your Rear Foot: To strike a blow, you must transfer your weight from the rear foot to the front foot. Keep your feet balanced and stable to maintain stability while moving by distributing your weight evenly between your feet.

Keep Your Feet Parallel and Your Hips Forward: When standing in the boxing stance, keep your feet parallel to each other. Your feet should be pointing straight ahead rather than angled inward or outward. Also, keep your hips forward to maintain body alignment and balance.

Maintain A Low Center Of Gravity: To have a solid boxing stance, you must keep the center of gravity low by bending your knees slightly. It helps maintain your balance, making moving around the ring easier and avoiding being knocked down by an opponent's punch.

Keep Your Hands Up: Your hands are your primary weapon in boxing. Keep them near your face and chin to prevent your opponent from landing a knockout punch. Keep your elbow close to your body and your lead hand slightly away to create an opening quickly.

Relax Your Shoulders: Tension in your shoulders can restrict your movement, making it much harder to dodge your opponent's punches. Ensure your shoulders are relaxed to execute roundhouse punches and hooks.

Keep Your Head Moving: When in the ring, you must keep moving your head to avoid punches by moving your head up, down, and to the sides. However, ensure your chin is tucked into your chest to prevent it from getting hit.

Stay Light on Your Feet: Stay light on your feet to keep your reaction time sharp. It means bouncing up and down and moving your feet quickly to be ready to throw a punch or dodge an oncoming blow.

Use Your Angles: Use angles to gain an advantage over your opponent. For example, an opening can be created by moving your feet at a diagonal angle instead of perfectly forward.

Practice Your Stance: Finally, practice is essential in boxing. You must practice maintaining and changing your stance to give your muscles the memory to maintain a proper posture, making it easier to adopt the perfect stance during your boxing matches.

Boxing can be thrilling and challenging, but with these tips from boxing experts, you can take your skills to the next level. From improving your balance and hand-eye coordination to developing mental toughness and staying hydrated, there are countless ways to boost your performance in the ring. Whether you're a beginner or a seasoned pro, the key is to stay focused and disciplined and never stop learning and growing as a boxer. Remember, practice makes perfect.

Stay dedicated and commit to honing your skills each day. You can reach your boxing goals with hard work, perseverance, and dedication. It's essential to take the necessary steps to prevent injury, stay hydrated and fueled, get enough rest, and practice visualization techniques to ensure you remain healthy in the ring and maximize your performance. Incorporating these basic boxing techniques, you'll be on your way to becoming a better boxer and champion.

Chapter 5: Punches and Counterpunches

"Float like a butterfly, sting like a bee." - Muhammad Ali

Boxing is not just about throwing punches. It is an intricate dance involving many strategies, footwork, and, most importantly, punches and counterpunches. These are essential elements that make boxing the sport it is today. In the ring, it's not only about the strength of your punches. It's about using your opponent's movements to land the perfect counterpunch. A successful boxer knows how to anticipate their opponent's next move and react accordingly. It's like a game of chess, where you must always be one step ahead of your opponent.

Punches and counterpunches are the building blocks of boxing, and mastering them will take you one step closer to becoming a great boxer. This chapter is divided into sections, each focusing on a particular punch or counterpunch. It explains the purpose of each punch and counterattack, the mechanics behind them, common mistakes to avoid, and drills to help you improve. After reading this chapter, you'll be well on your way to becoming a master of the ring.

Introduction to Boxing Punches: The Basics and Safety Tips

Boxing punches are a fundamental skill that must be mastered for a successful match. However, it is not about throwing hard punches and defeating your opponent. Boxing punches involve a lot of technique and safety. Therefore, it's essential to know the basics of boxing punches and their purpose, the techniques involved, and safety tips to reduce your risk of injury.

Purpose of Punches

Boxing punches aim to score points or knock out your opponent. Scoring points is a technical way of winning a boxing match. A boxer must throw the right punches accurately and effectively to score points. However, a knockout is the most popular way a fighter wins a game. To knock out your opponent, you must deliver a powerful punch that can cause the opponent to fall or lose consciousness. Knockouts don't only come from power punches. They can come from repeated punches that fatigue the opponent and leave him vulnerable.

Safety Tips for Punching

Boxing punches can be dangerous if not done correctly. Therefore, safety should always come first when practicing boxing punches. Here are some tips to help keep you safe while practicing:

1. Always wear the required safety gear, such as gloves, headgear, mouthguard, elbow pads, and knee pads, to minimize the risk of injury.

2. Warm up before starting any punches to prevent muscle injuries. Stretch before and after a workout to keep your muscles relaxed.

3. During practice, always have a trainer supervise your punching form to ensure safety and prevent bad habits.

4. Always take your time, and don't overdo it by rushing. Take breaks between punches and listen to your body.

Basic Punch Mechanics

The basic punch mechanics in boxing include the jab, cross, uppercut, and hook. Understanding basic punching techniques is integral to developing your skills and avoiding injuries. The jab is a quick straight punch delivered with the lead hand. The cross is a straight punch delivered with the rear hand. The uppercut is a punch delivered to your opponent's chin from below by bending the legs and the trunk. Last, the hook is a sideways punch by bending the arm at an obtuse angle and hitting the opponent's side of the face with the knuckles.

Punch mechanics use proper punch alignment, stance, and footwork. Proper punch alignment consists of the correct posture for maximum power and accuracy. Boxing stance means standing with the feet shoulder-width apart with one foot slightly ahead of the other. As for footwork, it is using your feet not only to move but also to generate power.

Learning the basics of boxing punches and their purpose is crucial in becoming a great boxer. It includes understanding the safety tips for executing punches, basic punch mechanics, and maintaining the correct posture and alignment. By practicing and perfecting these basic skills, you can become a better boxer, reducing the risk of injury. Always keep safety in mind and listen to your body while training. Developing your boxing punch skill requires patience, dedication, and practice.

Mastering the Jab: A Guide for Beginners

A jab can make all the difference in a fight.
Alain Delmas (France), CC BY-SA 3.0 <http://creativecommons.org/licenses/by-sa/3.0/>, via Wikimedia Commons: https://commons.wikimedia.org/wiki/File:Jab3.jpg

The jab is one of the most basic punches to master. It might seem like a simple punch, but a well-executed jab can make all the difference to the outcome of a fight. A quick and effective jab can keep your opponent at bay, set up other punches, and, most importantly, score points. This section reviews everything you need to know about the jab, including its definition, purpose, execution, common mistakes to avoid, and training drills to improve your technique.

Definition and Purpose of a Jab

The jab is a quick, straight punch thrown with the lead hand in boxing. Its primary purpose is to keep your opponent at bay, allowing you to create distance and set up other punches. The jab effectively scores points and disrupts your opponent's rhythm. It's the most common punch in boxing, with numerous variations, including the double jab, the triple jab, and the jab to the body.

Step-By-Step Set Up and Execution of the Jab

To execute a jab correctly, follow these steps:

1. Start with your feet shoulder-width apart, your knees slightly bent, and your weight evenly distributed.
2. Your lead hand should be held at chin level, with your elbow tucked in and your wrist straight.
3. When you're ready to jab, step forward with your lead foot and extend your arm straight out, turning your wrist slightly as you do so.
4. Your shoulder and hips should rotate slightly to generate power but don't overextend your arm or lean forward.
5. Once your jab lands, quickly retract your arm back to your chin, avoiding unnecessary movements.
6. Keep your non-lead hand up to protect your face, and stay light on your feet, ready to move or throw another punch.

Common Mistakes to Avoid

Here are some common mistakes to avoid when executing a jab:

1. Extending your arm too far can leave you vulnerable and decrease power. Keep your arm straight but not fully developed, and practice retracting it quickly to avoid this mistake.
2. Reaching with your jab takes away power and exposes you to counterpunches. Instead, step forward into the punch while keeping your chin tucked down.
3. Not stepping forward enough when you jab can result in a weak or ineffective punch. Instead, quickly step forward with your lead foot before throwing your jab.

---

4. Telegraphing your jab by positioning your body or hand before throwing it is a common mistake. Refrain from allowing your opponent to anticipate your movement and prepare a defense.

Training Drills to Improve Your Jab

The jab is the most important punch in boxing and should be the focus of your training drills. A good jab will set up your other punches and help you control the fight. Here are some exercises to improve your jab technique:

Wall Jab Drill: Stand a few feet away from a wall and practice throwing jabs at it. Focus on the set-up and execution of the punch, ensuring to avoid common mistakes. Visualize an opponent and practice your techniques without actually hitting anything.

Shadowboxing: Shadowboxing will help you get comfortable with throwing jabs and other punches without the pressure of a real opponent.

Speed Bag: Working on your speed and accuracy on the speed bag is a great way to practice throwing jabs quickly and accurately.

1-2-3 Drill: Throw a jab, then follow it with a right hand. Finish with a left hook to the body. Repeat this drill for 3 minutes, rest for 1 minute, and repeat three times.

Double-end bag drill: Throw a jab at the top, then quickly move to the bottom of the bag and throw another jab. Repeat this for 30 seconds, rest for 30 seconds, and repeat three times.

Focus Mitt Drill: Have a partner hold a focus mitt or punching pad in front of their face and throw jabs at it while moving around them. Repeat this for 3 minutes, rest for 1 minute, and repeat three times.

Partner Drill: Sparring with a partner can help you apply what you've learned in an actual fighting situation. Start slow, focus on technique, and gradually increase the intensity as you improve.

Mastering the Cross in Boxing: A Step-By-Step Guide

A cross is one of the most effective punches in boxing.
Delmas Alain, CC BY-SA 3.0 <https://creativecommons.org/licenses/by-sa/3.0>, via Wikimedia Commons: https://commons.wikimedia.org/wiki/File:Retrait4color.jpg

Boxing may look effortless when you watch professionals in the ring, but executing each move requires a lot of hard work, skill, and strength. A cross is one of the most effective punches in boxing and can change the game in seconds. Therefore, it's an essential technique every boxer should master to become a formidable opponent in the ring. This section looks closely at the definition, purpose, execution, common mistakes, and training drills to improve your cross in boxing.

Definition and Purpose of a Cross

A cross, also known as a straight, is a power punch thrown from your rear hand, usually your right hand if you're right-handed or vice versa if you're left-handed. The purpose of the cross is to create distance between you and your opponent while simultaneously delivering a powerful punch to their head or body. In addition, the cross often sets up other punches, like a hook or an uppercut.

Step-By-Step Set Up and Execution of the Cross

To execute a cross, follow these steps:

1. Position your feet shoulder-width apart with your left foot slightly forward and the right foot slightly back.

2. Next, keep your fists raised, elbows tucked close to your body, and your chin down to protect yourself from counterattacks.

3. From this position, use your hips, core, and shoulder to rotate your body as you straighten your back arm to extend your punch toward your target.

4. Remember to twist your wrist so that your knuckles are vertical when making contact with your opponent.

5. Last, recover by quickly returning your backhand to its original position, close to your face.

Common Mistakes to Avoid

Many people throw their cross without a set-up. However, a successful cross requires more than just a powerful punch. It must be timed correctly and using your entire body. Here are other common mistakes to avoid:

1. **Not Practicing with the Correct Weight:** The cross is a powerful punch, and if you're not used to throwing it with the proper weight, you won't generate the same power when in a fight. Use a heavy bag that can take the punishment and that you're comfortable throwing your punches with the proper weight.

2. **Not Keeping Your Guard Up:** Remember to keep your chin down, tuck in your elbows when throwing the cross, and be prepared for a counterpunch.

3. **Throwing Wild Punches:** This mistake will quickly get you knocked out in a fight. Instead, keep your punches tight and controlled, and only throw them when you have an opening.

4. **Not Following through with Your Punches:** Extend your arm fully, snap your wrists when you throw the punch, and follow through with your entire body.

5. **Not Staying Balanced:** Keep your feet planted firmly on the ground when you throw it. Additionally, keep your body loose and relaxed so you can quickly shift your weight from one foot to the other.

Training Drills to Improve Your Cross

Like any boxing technique, mastering the cross requires consistent practice. To improve your cross, here are some training drills to practice:

1. **Jab-Cross-Slip Drill:** Stand in your boxing stance with your left hand in front of you and your right hand at your chin. Jab with your left hand, then immediately cross with your right. As you cross, slip to the side so that you are no longer in front of your opponent to avoid getting hit by their counterpunch. Repeat this drill for 30 seconds.

2. **Jab-Jab-Cross Drill:** In the same position as the first drill, with your left hand out and your right hand at your chin. Jab twice with your left hand, then cross with your right. As you cross, step forward to be in front of your opponent. This way, you can land your punch and set up a follow-up attack. Repeat this drill for 30 seconds.

3. **Jab-Cross-Hook Drill:** In the same position as the first two drills, with your left hand out and your right hand at your chin. Jab with your left hand, then immediately cross with your right. As you cross, throw a hook with your left hand. You will catch your opponent off guard and land a powerful punch. Repeat this drill for 30 seconds.

The Art of the Hook: Improve Your Boxing Skills

A hook is a punching technique used to hit opponents from the side.
Alain Delmas (France), CC BY-SA 3.0 <http://creativecommons.org/licenses/by-sa/3.0/>, via Wikimedia Commons: https://commons.wikimedia.org/wiki/File:Lecon_crochet.jpg

A hook is a powerful punch combined with speed, accuracy, and technique. Whether you are a novice or a seasoned boxer, it is a great tool to have in your arsenal. This section discusses the definition and purpose of a hook, a step-by-step guide on how to set up and execute a hook, common mistakes to avoid, and training drills to improve your hook.

Definition and Purpose of a Hook

A hook is a punching technique in boxing to hit an opponent from the side, either to the head or body. It is an effective punch requiring excellent timing and coordination. The hook aims to deliver a decisive blow while maintaining control and accuracy. A properly executed hook can differentiate between winning and losing a fight.

Step-By-Step Set Up and Execution of the Hook

Successfully executing a hook requires patience and practice. Here is a step-by-step guide on how to set up and execute the hook:

1. Stand in a boxing stance facing your opponent.
2. Shift your weight to your back foot while keeping your elbow close to your body.
3. Pivot on the ball of your foot and turn your hip towards your opponent while swinging your arm in a circular motion.
4. Aim for your target's temple, cheek, or ribs, and land the punch with the knuckles of your middle and index fingers.
5. Always keep your other arm up to protect yourself, and be prepared for counterattacks.

Common Mistakes to Avoid

While a hook is a powerful and effective punch, it is essential to avoid inevitable common mistakes:

1. **Not Turning Your Body Enough**: You must turn your whole body and hip during the punch to generate maximum power.
2. **Not Keeping the Elbow Close to Your Body**: It decreases the power of your punch and makes it easier for your opponent to block or counter.
3. **Not Pivoting on the Ball of Your Foot**: You must pivot on the ball of your foot to generate enough power for the punch to land effectively.

---

4. **Not Aiming for the Correct Target:** You must aim for your target's temple, cheek, or ribs to land the punch with maximum power.

5. **Hitting Too High or Too Low:** Always aim for the correct target to ensure maximum power and accuracy.

6. **Leaving Yourself Vulnerable to Counterattacks:** Always keep your other arm up to protect yourself from counterattacks.

Training Drills to Improve Your Hook

You can do several drills to improve the accuracy and power of your hook. Here are a few examples:

1. **Jump Rope:** Jumping rope is a great way to improve footwork and coordination. Focus on moving quickly and smoothly while jumping rope; it will help you develop the footwork necessary to throw accurate and powerful hooks.

2. **Punching Mitts:** Punching mitts are a great way to improve accuracy and power with your punches. Focus on throwing accurate and powerful punches while working with punching mitts; it will help transfer those skills into the ring.

3. **Reflex Ball:** A reflex ball is an excellent tool for developing hand-eye coordination. Focus on hitting the ball as quickly as possible; it will help transfer those skills into the ring.

4. **Heavy Bag:** One of the best ways to improve your hooks is to practice on a heavy bag. A heavy bag helps you develop power and accuracy with your hooks. You should focus on throwing your hooks with evil intent to knock your opponent out.

5. **Shadowboxing:** Shadowboxing is a great way to work on your technique without having an opponent present. It would be best if you focused on throwing accurate and powerful punches. Shadowboxing helps you develop the muscle memory to throw real and powerful hooks in the ring.

A hook is a technique that takes time and practice to master. Incorporating the hook into your training improves your overall boxing skills and gives you an edge in the ring. Remember to focus on your technique, aim for the right target, and always protect yourself. With these tips and training drills, you will be on your way to throwing powerful hooks like a professional boxer. Keep practicing, and never give up on your boxing journey.

How to Master the Uppercut Punch

An uppercut can deliver a knockout blow.

The uppercut punch is a powerful tool to add to your boxing arsenal. This punch is designed to deliver a knockout blow and is handy during a fight. However, correctly delivering an uppercut punch takes great skill and practice. This section guides you through the definition, purpose, and execution of the uppercut punch. Also provided are tips on avoiding common mistakes and training drills to improve your uppercut.

Definition and Purpose of an Uppercut

The uppercut punch is a short punch thrown upward toward the opponent's chin or torso. The uppercut delivers a knockout blow by taking advantage of the opponent's guard. Most boxers use the uppercut when the opponent is leaning forward or trying to make a move. This punch is very effective when the opponent attempts to close in on you.

Step-By-Step Set Up and Execution of the Uppercut

Here's how to properly execute the uppercut punch:

1. Stand in your boxing stance with your feet shoulder-width apart and your chin down.

2. Shift your weight to your back foot and pivot on the ball of that foot. It gives you power and leverage for the punch.

3. Keeping your elbow close to your body, throw the punch up with the knuckles of your middle and index fingers.

4. Aim for the opponent's chin or solar plexus and put your body into it.

5. Return to your stance after throwing the punch and immediately be prepared for a counterattack.

Common Mistakes to Avoid

Out of all the punches, the uppercut is often one of the most misused or over-applied. Here are some common mistakes to avoid:

1. **Rushing:** Take your time, and don't rush the punch. Ensure you set up the punch correctly before executing it.

2. **Reaching:** Wait to reach for your opponent with the punch. Keep it close to your body, and pivot on the ball of your foot for power and leverage.

3. **Lowering The Guard:** Always keep your chin down and your guard up. An exposed chin could be a potential target for a counterpunch.

4. **Not Loading:** Load up the punch by shifting your weight to your back foot before throwing it.

5. **Dropping Your Elbow:** Keep your elbow close to your body as you throw the punch. It increases the power of the punch and avoids getting countered.

Training Drills to Improve Your Uppercut

To perfect your uppercut punch, incorporate the following training drills into your routine:

1. **Fist Movements:** Practice moving your fist from the guard to the uppercut position and back again. Keep your hand close to your body as you move it.

2. **Sparring Partner:** Find a partner and practice throwing the uppercut on focus pads or heavy bags. The goal is to set up and execute the punch properly.

3. **Shadow Boxing:** Practice throwing the uppercut in front of a mirror or without one. Focus on setting up correctly and throwing the punch with proper form and power.

4. **Practice Standalone Uppercuts:** Do the uppercut punch independently and pay attention to details. Focus on your form, power, and timing. The more attention you pay to the elements, the better your uppercut will become.

5. **Follow Up with Combinations:** Combine uppercuts with other punches after perfecting the form. It helps you learn to use the punch with different shots.

How to Perfect Your Counterpunches in Boxing

Counterpunches can help you deflect your opponent's punches.
Delmas Alain, CC BY-SA 3.0 <https://creativecommons.org/licenses/by-sa/3.0>, via Wikimedia Commons: https://commons.wikimedia.org/wiki/File:Retrait2color.jpg

The great boxer Muhammad Ali was known for his swift footwork and powerful counterpunching. In a sport like boxing, anticipating and countering your opponent's moves can give you a significant advantage. Counterpunch is a strategic move to deflect and counter your opponent's punches while conserving your energy and maximizing your chances of landing a punch. This section discusses the definition and purpose of a counterpunch, step-by-step set-up and execution, common mistakes to avoid, and training drills to improve your counterpunching skills.

Definition and Purpose of a Counterpunch

Counterpunch is a punch thrown after dodging an incoming punch from your opponent. The counterpunch aims to exploit your opponent's mistakes by catching them off guard and generating power. It allows the counterpuncher to take control of the round convincingly. Effective counterpunching is all about timing and precision.

Step-By-Step Set-Up and Execution of the Counterpunch

Remember, the counterpunch should be used sparingly. Here are the basic steps for setting up and executing a counterattack:

1. Step out of the way of your opponent's punch as you lean slightly to one side and put your chin down; this puts you in a position to throw a counterpunch.

2. Bring your guard back up and your fist forward as you pivot on the ball of your foot.

3. Use power and speed to land your punch while keeping your elbows close to your body and chin down.

4. Return to the guard position when the counterpunch is thrown.

When an incoming punch is thrown, move your upper body, head, and feet away from the incoming punch. If the incoming punch is a jab, use a slip and slide to the outside of the jab and deliver a counterpunch to the head. For incoming hooks, pivot your feet, move your hips, and throw a counterpunch to the face or body. For incoming uppercuts, lean back to one side and throw a counterpunch to the head or body.

Common Mistakes to Avoid

When attempting a counterpunch, avoid the following common mistakes:

1. **Being Too Slow:** Remember to time your counter punch just right. Waiting too long to throw your punch gives your opponent time to recover and launch another punch.

2. **Not Keeping The Balance:** Keep your balance by keeping your feet, knees, and hips aligned; this helps you move quickly and throw a powerful counterpunch.

3. **Not Anticipating The Opponent's Move:** Always look for the signs of an incoming punch and anticipate your opponent's next move.

4. **Not Maintaining Proper Form**: Keep your elbows in, chin down, and guard up to help you move quickly and maintain balance.

Training Drills to Improve Your Counterpunching Skills

The following are some training drills to help improve your counterpunching skills:

1. Double Slip Drill: This drill involves slipping two jabs before throwing a counterpunch.
2. Jab/Cross Drill: This drill involves slipping a jab and counters with a cross punch.
3. Hook/Uppercut Drill: This drill involves slipping a hook and countering with an uppercut punch.
4. Shadowboxing Drill: This drill involves shadowboxing and working on your timing
5. Double Uppercut Drill: This drill involves slipping two uppercuts before throwing a counterpunch.

Regularly practicing these drills improves your timing, power, and accuracy and helps you to achieve an effective counterpunch. In addition, with these tips and tricks, you can maximize your chances of landing a powerful punch.

This chapter provided an overview of the various punches and counterpunches in boxing and some training drills to improve your skills. From jabs and crosses to hooks and uppercuts, you've learned the basics of throwing each punch and how to effectively time and execute a counterpunch. With practice and dedication, you can produce an effective counterpunch, taking advantage of your opponent's mistakes and increasing your chances of winning the round. Good luck.

Chapter 6: Defense Tips and Techniques

While throwing punches is the flashy side of the sport, the art of defense is as important. A good defense can help you avoid getting hit and conserve energy for when it counts. Skilled boxers can slip punches, weave through opponents, and use footwork to dodge incoming attacks. It's not easy, but the result is well worth it. A successful defense can give you the edge to come out of a brutal battle victorious.

This chapter focuses on defensive boxing tips and techniques. It instructs how to block and deflect various punches, defend your head, use the proper footwork, bob, weave, slip, clinch, roll, parry, and pivot. These critical elements of defensive boxing put you in a prime position to win. The fight is won or lost in the details; mastering these skills can make all the difference.

Defensive Blocking

Defensive blocking can be used for an offensive strategy.

Boxing can be an exhilarating sport, but it is dangerous. A well-timed punch can abruptly end a match, so fighters must master the art of defense. Defensive blocking is as vital as an excellent offensive strategy. This section discusses two essential boxing techniques, deflecting punches and protecting your head. Whether a seasoned professional or a novice, these techniques will keep you safe and extend your fighting career.

Deflecting Punches

Deflecting punches is a crucial defensive blocking technique every fighter should master. It involves using your hand or forearm to redirect the opponent's punch, making it miss its target. When done correctly, deflecting punches can disrupt the opponent's rhythm, waste their energy, and create an opening for a counterattack. Here are some tips for perfecting this technique:

1. **Maintain a Relaxed Stance:** Fighting with a tense stance tires you out quickly. Instead, keep your body relaxed, maintain a low center of gravity, and stay light on your feet. If you remain alert, your reflexes will be quicker, allowing you to sense better and redirect incoming punches.

2. **Use the Forearm:** A firm forearm is an excellent tool for deflecting punches. Keep your arms in a guard position and use the forearm to brush away any incoming hook or jab. The forearm should be angled to absorb the punch's force and redirect it away from your head or body.

3. **Keep Your Eyes on Your Opponent's Shoulders:** The torso initiates all the punches. Keeping your eyes fixed on your opponent's shoulders, you predict the direction of the punch and prepare accordingly. When you see the shoulder tense, you know a punch is coming, and use the appropriate defensive blocking technique to avoid it.

4. **Use a Deflection Technique:** Depending on the punch's angle and direction, you can use several deflection techniques. The most common is the parry, block, and slap. If the punch comes from high, use a parry to deflect it. If the punch is coming from low, then use a block. If the punch is coming from an angle, use a slap to deflect it.

Protecting Your Head

Protecting your head is the most vital defensive blocking technique in boxing. A blow to the head can lead to a knockout, brain damage, or death. Here are some tips for protecting your head:

1. **Keep Your Guard Up:** Keep your hands close to your face and your elbows tucked in. This stance shields your head from punches. The ideal guard position is with your chin down, elbows in, and fists up around the face.

2. **Keep the Ideal Distance:** An excellent way to protect your head is by keeping the proper distance between you and your opponent. If you are too far away, it will be hard to land punches. If you are too close, your opponent will have a clear shot at your head. Therefore, the ideal distance is just outside the range of your opponent's punches.

3. **Practice Head Movement:** Good head movement involves ducking, slipping, and bobbing. Practice these techniques to become more elusive and avoid being hit. In addition, it's essential to keep your head moving so that the opponent cannot predict where you'll move and set up their punch accordingly.

4. **Know When to Clinch:** If your opponent's punches are too fast or too strong, then clinch. Clinching is holding your opponent in

a close embrace to stop them from hitting you. Grabbing the opponent's arms and holding them close to your body prevents them from throwing punches.

Footwork Basics of Boxing: Moving Around the Ring with Speed and Precision

Footwork is one of the most critical aspects of the sport. Proper footwork allows boxers to move quickly and efficiently around the ring, throwing effective punches while avoiding their opponents' attacks. This section looks closely at some basic footwork techniques boxers use when moving around the ring. It covers everything from basic stance and balance to shifting weight and adjusting foot position for different punches. Whether you are a seasoned pro or a beginner, mastering these basics is essential for success in the ring.

Getting into Stance

Before moving around the ring, you must get into the proper stance. It means standing with your feet shoulder-width apart, with your toes pointed slightly outward. Your knees should be slightly bent, and your weight should be evenly distributed on both feet. You can adjust your stance from here depending on your opponent's position and movements.

Professional boxers often adjust their stances to be more aggressive or defensive, depending on the situation. For example, if your opponent throws a lot of jabs, you might take a more defensive stance with your hands up and your chin tucked down. On the other hand, if you intend to throw a combination, you may adjust your stance to be slightly broader and more aggressive.

Moving around the Ring

Once you're in the proper stance, it's time to start moving. You can move forward, backward, and side to side by taking small, quick steps. Stay light on your feet and keep your knees bent to maintain balance and stability. Take short steps with your lead foot, using your back foot to propel yourself forward as needed. When moving backward, reverse this motion, taking small steps with your back foot and using your lead foot to push off. Lateral movement involves taking small steps to the side to avoid your opponent's punches or to get into a better position for your punches.

Balancing and Shifting Weight

As you move around the ring, you must maintain proper balance and shift your weight effectively. It involves keeping your weight centered over your feet and shifting it from foot to foot. For example, when throwing a punch with your lead hand, you turn your weight slightly to your lead foot while anchoring your back foot for stability. The same principle applies when throwing punches with your backhand. You shift your weight to the opposite side and use your lead foot for balance.

Adjusting Foot Position for Different Punches

Different punches require different foot positioning. For example, when throwing a jab, your lead foot should step forward slightly, giving you more reach for your punch. Your lead foot should pivot outward for a hook, allowing you to twist your body and generate more power behind your punch. Finally, for an uppercut, get close to your opponent, stepping forward with your lead foot to get in range.

Practicing Footwork

Like any skill, footwork requires practice to master. Spend time working on your footwork in the gym, focusing on moving quickly and efficiently around the ring. Practice different punches and foot positioning, getting comfortable with each movement and transition. You will throw more effective punches and easily avoid your opponent's attacks as you improve your footwork. Here are some drills to get you started:

1. **Shadowboxing:** Practice your footwork and punches on the heavy bag, focusing on speed, power, and accuracy.
2. **Reaction Drills:** Have a partner throw punches at varying speeds and angles. Practice shifting your weight, adjusting foot positioning, and dodging or blocking the punches.
3. **Speed Drills:** Time how fast you can move around the ring, practicing footwork drills at various speeds.
4. **Slip Drills:** Have your partner throw jabs and crosses at you, and practice slipping the punches or dodging to the side.

Head Movement Techniques

Boxing is not just about throwing punches but also knowing how to avoid them. Therefore, head movement techniques in boxing are essential if you want to be a good boxer. These techniques can help you avoid punches, counterattack, and move confidently in the ring. This section discusses in detail these techniques and how to master them.

1. **Bobbing:** Bobbing is a technique that moves the head up and down while keeping the feet rooted to the ground. It is an excellent technique to avoid hooks and overhand punches. To perform this technique, keep your knees slightly bent, and move your head up and down fluidly. Keep your hands up to defend yourself against jabs and straights. Practice bobbing by having a partner throw punches at you while you bob and weave to avoid them.

2. **Weaving:** Weaving is a technique of moving your head from side to side while bending your knees. It is an effective technique to avoid straight punches. To perform this technique, move your head to the left and right while keeping your hands up to defend against hooks. You can practice weaving by having a partner throw straight punches at you while you weave to avoid them.

3. **Slipping:** Slipping is a technique of moving the head to the side to avoid a punch. It is an excellent technique for avoiding jabs and straights. To perform this technique, move your head to the left or the right while bending your knees. Practice slipping by having a partner throw jabs and straights at you while you slip to avoid them.

4. **Rolling:** Rolling is a technique of moving your head in a circular motion to avoid punches. It is an effective technique for preventing hooks and overhand punches. To perform this technique, move your head in a circular motion while keeping your hands up to defend against jabs and straights. Practice rolling by having a partner throw hooks and overhand punches at you while you move to avoid them.

5. **Parrying:** Parrying is a technique using your hands to deflect a punch. It is an excellent technique for avoiding jabs and straights. To perform this technique, use your front hand to deflect a jab or straight by pushing it to the side. Practice parrying by having a partner throw jabs and straights at you while you dodge to deflect them.

6. **Pivoting:** Pivoting is a technique that involves turning your body to avoid a punch. It is an effective technique for preventing hooks and overhand punches. To perform this technique, pivot on your front foot to turn your body to the left or the right. Keep

your hands up to defend against jabs and straights. Practice shifting by having a partner throw hooks and overhand punches at you while you pivot to avoid them.

Mastering head movement techniques in boxing is essential to be a good boxer. These techniques can help you avoid punches and counterattack effectively. Bobbing, weaving, slipping, rolling, dodging, and pivoting are essential techniques every aspiring boxer should master. Practice these techniques regularly with a partner to improve your skills and your confidence in the ring. Remember to keep your hands up at all times, stay calm, and move with fluidity and grace.

Clinching for Defense: How to Use Your Arms and Control Distance

Clinching is a valuable defensive tool.

In boxing, sometimes you need to use your entire body to defend yourself, including your arms and clinching skills. A clinch is when you grab your opponent's body to control their movement and reduce potential damage. Clinching can be a valuable defensive tool. This section explores two critical aspects of clinching, using your arms for defense and controlling distance in the clinch.

Using Your Arms for Defense

Your arms are a crucial component to successful clinching. When your opponent is attacking, use your arms to protect your head and body. For example, keep your elbows in and your hands up around your face. If your opponent tries to hit you, your head and body are protected.

When in the clinch, your arms should grab your opponent's body. Keep your elbows in tight and press your body into theirs. You can control their movements and restrict the space they have to move around you. Use your arms to block your opponent's knees, which can be very effective against fighters who try to knee you in the clinch.

Another excellent use for your arms is creating space when needed. For example, if you are in a tight clinch, and your opponent controls your movement, use your arms to push them away. It creates distance between you and your opponent, giving you room to move and defend yourself.

Controlling Distance in the Clinch

Controlling distance is a fundamental aspect of clinching. You must know how to get close to your opponent and stay there without giving them too much space to move around you. The key is taking small steps and making minor adjustments to your stance and body position. When first entering the clinch, take small steps toward your opponent. Get your head and body close to theirs, and wrap your arms around their body. Once you control their movement, take small steps backward or sideways to maintain your position.

If your opponent tries to move away from you, use your arms to pull them back. Keep your elbows tight to your body and use your chest and shoulders to press into theirs. You will control their movement and keep them close. Sometimes your opponent will push you back or move away from you. In these situations, be patient, and make minor adjustments to your stance and body position. Keep your arms up, ready to defend, and wait for the right opportunity to strike.

Clinching can be a very effective defensive tool when used correctly. Using your arms for defense and controlling distance in the clinch are two critical aspects of successful clinching. Practice these skills with a partner to improve your technique and control. Remember to keep your elbows tight and use your chest and shoulders to control your opponent's movements. Clinching can become a valuable component of your fighting repertoire with some practice.

Essential Boxing Defense Tips from Pro Fighters

Whether a beginner or an experienced boxer, defense is essential to your training regimen. Proper defense can minimize the damage inflicted by an opponent's punches and tire them out. Some of the best boxing defense tips from pro fighters you can incorporate into your training are listed below.

1. **Keep Your Hands Up:** One of the most basic and essential aspects of boxing defense is to keep your hands up in front of your face. Your hands should be positioned to cover your nose and chin while providing enough room to see your opponent's punches. This defensive technique blocks punches coming directly at you and from an angle.

2. **Stay Alert and Keep Your Eyes Open:** While fighting, you must maintain your focus and stay alert. Watch your opponent closely and look for signs of an attack. This way, you can plan your moves based on your opponent's. Keeping your eyes open is an essential skill you must develop.

3. **Boxing Stance:** A solid boxing stance can help you defend yourself better during fights. Keep your feet shoulder-width apart, your left foot forward (if you're right-handed), your knees slightly bent, and your hands up to protect your face. Use your left hand to block your opponent's jab and your right hand for power punches. Last, keep your elbows close to your ribs to make it harder for your opponent to hit your body.

4. **Counterattack:** The best defense is a good offense. When you see an opening, take full advantage of it. Throw a counter punch and keep your opponent backtracking, relieving the pressure on you and helping you gain momentum. When you get the opportunity to counterattack, be quick and aggressive.

5. **Partner Drills:** Practice with your partner to learn to defend yourself. Do partner drills and learn to block their punches and land your punches. Practicing with a partner develops timing and reflexes. In a real fight, you must anticipate your opponent's moves and get your punches in before they do. Getting hands-on

experience with a partner will develop this skill.

6. **Focus on Timing:** Timing is an essential skill for boxing defense. You must time your blocks and counterpunches perfectly to avoid getting hit. Focus on developing your timing and reflexes by doing live drills with a partner. Remember, you can only sometimes rely on your guard to protect you. You must be alert and time your blocks correctly to defend yourself effectively.

7. **Look Out for Opponent's Combinations:** Paying attention to your opponent's combinations is essential. If you notice them throwing a variety of punches, be prepared to block them all. Learn to defend against combinations by doing drills with a partner and to ensure you stay alert during your fights. Learn to anticipate your opponent's moves and react quickly.

Defense is vital for your boxing performance. Developing a good defense to avoid taking unnecessary hits is crucial. This chapter covered defensive blocking, deflecting punches, bobbing and weaving, slipping, clinching, rolling, and parrying. It shared some of the best boxing defense tips from pro fighters to incorporate into your training regime. Remember to keep your hands up, stay alert, and keep your eyes open. Always move your head, focus on your footwork, be ready to counterattack, and practice partner drills. These tips will improve your defense and lead you to success.

Chapter 7: 13 Pro Combinations You Didn't Know

The art of boxing is not only about throwing punches. It's combining them the most strategically. The right combination of punches can differentiate between victory and defeat. A well-executed combination involves precision, accuracy, and timing. It's like a choreographed dance where each step must be taken with total focus and determination. Combining punches can be challenging, especially when facing a skilled opponent, but it's a thing of beauty once mastered.

Mastering combinations should be high on your priority list to have a shot at becoming a boxing champion. This chapter teaches the basics, intermediate, advanced combos, and some finishing moves to help you gain the upper hand in a fight. In addition, it contains step-by-step instructions on each combination so you can practice and hone your skills until they become second nature. After all, practice makes perfect.

Basic Boxing Combinations to Boost Your Skills

Every boxer is familiar with the importance of mastering the basics. Basic boxing combinations are the bread and butter of boxing that help you gain the upper hand in the ring. You must work on your technique and form to execute the perfect punch, block, and counterattack. This section guides you through the essential combinations to take your boxing skills to the next level.

Jab and Cross Combination

JAB   CROSS

Jab and cross combination

This is one of the most common and effective boxing combinations. Start with a quick and sharp jab to your opponent's face, followed by a powerful cross punch with your dominant hand. Keep your guard up after the cross punch to avoid retaliation from your opponent. Practice this combination with a speed or heavy bag to improve your timing and coordination.

Hook and Uppercut Combination

The hook and uppercut combination is a great way to surprise your opponent. Start with a quick hook punch with your dominant hand to your opponent's head or body, followed by an uppercut with your other hand to catch them off guard. Keep your body balanced and grounded during the combination to avoid getting knocked out. Practice this combination on a heavy bag to improve your stamina and power.

Overhand Right Combo

Right overhand combination.
Alain Delmas (France), CC BY-SA 3.0 <http://creativecommons.org/licenses/by-sa/3.0/>, via Wikimedia Commons: https://commons.wikimedia.org/wiki/File:Drop5.jpg

The right overhand combination is a powerful punch that can knock your opponent down. Start with a jab to set up your punch, then throw a right overhand punch with your dominant hand directly to your opponent's head. This combination must be executed using the proper technique to avoid telegraphing your move. The key to this combination is to turn your hips and follow through with your shoulder during the punch.

One-Two-Three Combo

JAB   CROSS   HOOK

One-Two-Three Combo

The One-Two-Three combination is a staple in a boxer's arsenal. Start with a jab, followed by a cross punch, and finish with a hook punch to your opponent's head or body. Pivot your foot during the hook punch to add more power to your punch. This combination is perfect for taking down your opponent with a quick and powerful sequence of punches.

Mastering Intermediate Boxing Moves

Intermediate moves are critical for boxers to improve their performance in the ring. These moves involve combinations of punches requiring speed, agility, accuracy, and power. This section reveals three intermediate boxing moves to help you gain an edge over your opponent. Practicing these moves regularly on a heavy and speed bag to perfect your technique will make you unstoppable in the ring.

Left Hook and Overhand Right Combo

The left hook and right overhand combo is a powerful combination that can leave your opponent disoriented and off-balance. Start by throwing a left hook to the head or body, followed by a right overhand punch. Ensure you pivot your left foot as you throw the left hook. This movement helps increase the power of your punch by transferring your weight to the front foot. The right overhand should come as a surprise to your opponent, throwing them off balance. Remember to follow through with the strike to maximize the impact.

Lead Uppercut and Rear Uppercut Combination

LEAD UPPERCUT   REAR UPPERCUT

Lead and rear uppercut combination

A lead and rear uppercut combination is an effective inside-fighting move closing the distance with your opponent. Start by throwing a lead uppercut punch with your left hand and follow up with a rear uppercut with your right hand. The lead uppercut should focus on landing on the chin, while the rear uppercut should aim for the solar plexus or liver. Practice this combination with a speed or heavy bag to increase your accuracy and speed.

Double Hook and Uppercut Combo

The double hook and uppercut combo is a flashy and effective technique to confuse your opponent. Start by throwing a left hook to the body or head, follow it up with a right hook to the body or head, and end it with a left uppercut. Pivot your feet and rotate through the hips as you deliver the punches. The hooks should be aimed at the ribs or the temple, while the uppercut should aim at the chin. Practice this combo by imagining your opponent's movement and adjusting your punches accordingly.

Advanced Combos

Boxing combos are tricky to master, but they can take your game to the next level once you get the hang of it. The right combos can help you set the pace, create openings, and stun your opponents with quick power strikes. So, to advance your boxing game, it's time to work on advanced boxing combos. This section shares some of the most effective combos to elevate your game and keep your opponents on their toes.

Lead Right Hook and Rear Left Hook Combo

This combo starts with a lead right hook

The lead right hook and rear left hook combo is a powerful combination to close the distance and overwhelm your opponent. Start with a jab, create an opening, and follow it up with a lead right hook. Then, as your opponent's guard drops to defend against the lead hook, follow up with a rear left hook that can deliver a knockout. This combo requires good footwork and timing, so practicing it with a sparring partner is better.

Lead Right Uppercut and Rear Left Hook Combo

The lead right uppercut and rear left hook combo is another effective combination to catch your opponent off-guard. Start with a quick jab followed by a lead right uppercut. The uppercut should connect with your opponent's chin, leaving them stunned and open for a rear left hook. The left hook is a devastating punch that can knock your opponent out, so ensure you have good balance and stance before you attempt it.

Four-Punch Combination

The four-punch combination is worth trying for a more complex combo. This combo starts with a lead left hook, followed by a jab, a lead hook, and a cross. The first punch should create an opening for the jab, which sets up the lead hook. The final punch, the cross, delivers the knockout power shot that can end the fight. This combo requires good coordination and timing, so practicing it slowly and gradually adding speed is better.

Lead Right Straight and Rear Left Uppercut Combo

Start this combo with a right straight punch

The lead right straight and rear left uppercut combo is a variation of the previous combos and can be performed differently. Start with a lead right straight followed by a rear left uppercut. Then, the uppercut can be delivered to your opponent's chin or body, depending on their guard. This combo can be performed with different variations, including a left hook, a right hook, or a body shot.

Double Jab and Right Cross Combo

The double jab and right cross combo is a classic combination to control the fight's pace. Start with two quick jabs creating an opening for a powerful right cross. The double jab keeps your opponent on their toes and sets up your power shots. This combo requires good accuracy and speed, so practice your jabs and crosses before attempting it.

Knockout Techniques: Master These Finishing Moves

It's no secret that knockout punches can be the difference between winning and losing a fight. But, as a boxer, mastering finishing moves can give you the upper hand in ending the battle in your favor. This section looks at some of the most effective finishing moves in your arsenal.

Lead Left Hook and Rear Right Hook Combo

One of the most popular finishing moves in boxing is the lead left hook and rear right hook combo. This technique starts with a left-lead hook and a rear right hook to throw your opponent off balance and muddle their defense. The key to executing this combo is ensuring both punches are thrown with quick, fluid movements. Make sure to land your punches with precision and power to ensure a successful knockout.

Lead Left Uppercut, Rear Right Cross, and Lead Right Uppercut Combo

Another effective finishing move is the lead left uppercut, rear right cross, and lead right uppercut combo. This combination leads with a left uppercut, followed by a rear right cross, and finishing with a lead right uppercut. This combo is highly effective in close combat situations, as it allows you to land powerful punches even when your opponent has their guard up. Again, to ensure maximum impact, the key to executing this combo is maintaining good footwork and speed.

Six-Punch Combination

The six-punch combination is a powerful and complex finishing move involving six punches thrown quickly. This technique can be executed in several variations. The most common is a combination of two jabs, crosses, and hooks. This finishing move requires excellent timing and precision, so focusing on your technique and speed is essential when practicing. The six-punch combination is effective in wearing down your opponent and finding an opening for a knockout punch.

Body Shots

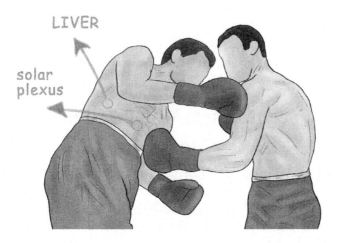

LIVER

solar
plexus

Body shots target the liver and solar plexus.

While many finishing moves focus on targeting your opponent's head, body shots can also be highly effective in securing a knockout. This technique targets your opponent's midsection, specifically their liver. A well-placed body shot can effectively weaken your opponent and set them up for a knockout punch to the head. To execute a successful body shot, aim for your opponent's midsection, and use your body weight to generate power and force behind your punch.

Feints and Fakes

Feints can distract your opponent

Last, another effective finishing move technique is using feints and fakes to distract and confuse your opponent. This technique pretends to throw a punch in one direction before throwing a knockout punch in another. It is a highly effective way to catch your opponent off guard and land a successful knockout punch. However, it's essential to be cautious when using this technique, as it requires a high skill level and can be risky.

Tips for Finding the Best Boxing Combinations

Boxing is a fascinating and challenging sport requiring much skill and endurance. One of the most important aspects of boxing is learning to use combinations effectively to gain an advantage over your opponent. Good boxing combinations require physical strength, strategic planning, and swift execution. This section provides excellent tips for finding the best boxing combinations to improve your boxing skills and dominate the ring.

Develop a Strong Foundation

Before practicing complicated boxing combinations, you must build a solid foundation that includes basic techniques like jabs, crosses, hooks, and uppercuts. These moves, when executed correctly, can devastate your opponent. Start with the basics and practice until you can perform these moves perfectly. Then, gradually move on to more complex combinations. Your initial combinations should be basic enough that you can execute them without thinking and become second nature.

Study Professional Boxing Matches

Watching professional boxing matches provides excellent opportunities to observe and learn from the best. When you watch these matches, take note of the combinations your favorite boxers use and try to recreate them during your training sessions. Feel free to pause the videos and practice the moves slowly to gain a clear understanding of how to execute them with precision.

Practice with a Partner

Practicing with a partner can help you improve your techniques.

Practicing with a partner is a great way to improve your boxing techniques. Find someone willing to collaborate on your training sessions and create various combinations. Start by throwing basic punches and gradually add more intricate moves once you feel more confident. Working with a partner helps improve your timing, accuracy, and speed.

Develop Your Style

A good boxer has a unique style. It takes time to develop your boxing style, but experimenting with different combinations and techniques creates a personal style that matches your physical abilities. Trying different combinations will help you to find the right moves that work for you in the ring. Of course, the best way to find your style is to practice, so spend enough time mastering the basics and learning new combinations.

Practice against Different Opponents

Once you've developed a few combinations, it's time to test them out against different opponents. You will understand the strengths and weaknesses of your technique and make necessary adjustments. Working with other opponents sharpens your reflexes, giving you an edge in the ring. The more opponents you practice against, the higher your chances of success.

Consistency Is Key

Consistency is vital to developing boxing skills. You must practice regularly to get the most out of your training sessions. Consistency helps build muscle memory, which is significant in executing complex techniques. A big part of success in the ring comes down to practice and repetition. Consistency will improve your boxing skills and give you the confidence to succeed in the ring.

Keep Your Combinations Simple

Keeping your combinations simple but effective is the key to success in the ring. You don't need a lot of fancy moves to win a fight; all you need is one or two powerful punches that will land and impact your opponent. So, keep it simple and stick with the basics. It's far more effective than executing complex combinations that might not work. A few well-executed punches can go a long way and make all the difference in the ring.

Mastering boxing combinations takes time, dedication, and patience. Remember to start with the basics and gradually move to more complicated moves. Watching professional boxing matches, working with a partner, and developing your style are ways to improve your boxing skills. Consistency is critical, and practice makes perfect. Stay focused, keep working hard, and you'll execute impressive combinations in no time.

Boxing is not only about throwing punches but also executing them precisely and accurately. Mastering the basic boxing combinations can help you become a skilled fighter. It's essential to start with the basics, work on your form and technique, and graduate to more complex combinations. Find a good boxing coach to guide you through these combinations and improve your skills. Remember, practice makes perfect, so keep training and pushing yourself to become your best boxer.

Chapter 8: Peek-A-Boo: Sparring Secrets of Pro Boxers

Boxing is an intense sport demanding physical fitness and mental agility. Pro boxers are known for their skill and technique, but what are their secrets regarding sparring?

The key to winning the match is not just brute strength but strategy and quick thinking. With thorough preparation and a determined attitude, anyone can learn the sparring secrets of pro boxers and become a champion. This chapter will start you on the path of sparring success.

This chapter explores the basics of sparring, discusses the right time to start sparring with an opponent, breaks down the technical aspects of sparring, and provides expert-level tips from the pros. From Mike Tyson's infamous "peek-a-boo" style to head movement and footwork, you'll be well prepared to take on your first match. Then, on your way to the sparring party, explore everything about sparring.

The Basics of Sparring

Sparring can help you improve your skills.

Sparring is a standard part of almost every combat sport and a great way to improve your skills. Whether learning martial arts or practicing kickboxing, sparring is essential to becoming a better fighter. This section covers sparring basics, providing everything you need to know to get started, from the benefits of sparring to the techniques.

Why You Should Spar

Sparring is integral to martial arts training because it exposes you to real-life situations. It allows you to practice your techniques against an opponent and learn to react in different situations. Additionally, sparring helps you improve your reflexes, timing, footwork, and endurance. With these benefits, sparring is essential to becoming a skilled fighter.

The Different Types of Sparring

Sparring can be broken down into different types, like hard, light, or technical. Hard sparring is the most intense form, where opponents fight at full power. In contrast, light sparring is less severe, with fighters only using 30%-60% of their strength. Finally, technical sparring focuses more on technique, where fighters practice specific moves and counters.

Tips for Beginners

Sparring can be intimidating, especially if facing someone more experienced than you. However, you can turn sparring into a valuable learning experience if you have the right mindset. Firstly, approach every sparring session with an open mind, ready to learn and improve. Secondly, always wear the proper safety gear, such as headgear, gloves, and shin guards. Last, don't hesitate to ask your coach or sparring partner for feedback after each session to help you identify areas you need to improve and track your progress.

The Right Time to Start Sparring

Are you an aspiring boxer waiting for the right time to start sparring? Sparring is essential to boxing training, preparing a fighter for real-life situations. However, it can be challenging to determine when it is the right time to start sparring. This section provides insight into when it is appropriate to start sparring and its benefits.

Getting the Basics Right

Before sparring, ensure you have learned and mastered the fundamental boxing techniques. For example, it would be best to have sound footwork, balance, and head movement to effectively evade your opponent's punches. Also, ensure you are comfortable with the stance and that your punches are accurate and robust. With a good grasp of these fundamentals, you can protect yourself and avoid getting injured during sparring.

Build Up Your Fitness Levels

It is imperative to have adequate fitness before sparring. Sparring is an intensive form of training requiring you to move continuously for a few rounds. It can be physically and mentally exhausting, and you must build your endurance to cope with the sparring demands. Therefore, start with some cardiovascular exercises to improve your cardiovascular fitness, such as jogging, skipping, or cycling.

Confidence Is Key

Having confidence before sparring is beneficial. Remember, you will face an opponent trying to hit you. Therefore, being confident with your techniques and mentally tough is essential. Your coach can mentally prepare you to deal with the stress and anxiety of sparring. Moreover, a little self-confidence will make you enjoy sparring and bring out your best.

Spar with Similar Ability Levels

As a beginner, sparring with boxers with similar abilities is essential. In addition, sparring with someone with more experience will help you because they can teach you a lot. However, sparring with someone above your skill level can be risky and intimidating, affecting your confidence. Therefore, spar with someone at your own level and slowly progress to a more challenging opponent.

Learn from Sparring

Last, sparring is an opportunity to learn from mistakes and improve your technique. Closely watch your opponent's moves and learn to counter them. Try different combinations and methods and test them out during sparring. Your coach will give feedback on your performance and suggest improvement areas.

Sparring is an essential part of boxing training but requires preparation and timing. Ensure you have learned the fundamentals, built your fitness, developed confidence, spar with similar-ability boxers, and learned from sparring. Remember, with good preparation, sparring becomes an enjoyable and beneficial part of your training, which will help you achieve your boxing goals.

Technical Aspects of Sparring

Sparring sharpens your techniques, improves confidence, and hones your reflexes. The technical aspects of sparring make it effective. Knowing the details, from your stance to your gaze, body movement, and technique, can help you become a better boxer. Let's delve into the technical considerations of sparring.

Stance

The stance you take when sparring is crucial. The correct stance provides a good balance, essential for maintaining stability while sparring. The stance helps you move in and out of range efficiently while keeping your guard up. A good stance includes keeping your feet shoulder-width apart, your head and shoulders relaxed, and your knees slightly bent.

Footwork

Footwork helps you move around quickly and effectively to dodge and evade attacks while setting up your own. A good footwork technique includes:

1. Keeping your weight on the balls of your feet.

2. Shifting your weight from one foot to another.

3. Using small and quick steps to move around.

Striking Techniques

Striking is the primary technique in sparring, and mastering the striking methods can make a huge difference in your ability to spar. An excellent striking technique includes proper form, timing, and accuracy. Focus on controlling your punches, kicks, and other strikes. Your striking techniques should be faster and more complex than your opponent's to keep them on their toes.

Defense Techniques

Defense is an essential aspect of sparring, helping you to avoid getting hit by your opponent. There are various defense techniques, including blocking, dodging, and parrying. A good defense involves:

1. Keeping your hands up.

2. Blocking with your arms and legs.

3. Using your footwork to move out of range.

Like with striking, keeping your defense tight and under control is vital. When sparring, you should always be ready to defend yourself.

Counters and Combination Techniques

Counterattacks and combination techniques help you gain the upper hand in sparring. Combining different methods, such as punches and kicks, can throw your opponent off balance, and counterattacks can strategically counteract your opponent's movements. A good counterattack and combination technique involves timing your attacks efficiently and using various techniques to keep your opponent guessing.

Sparring has many critical technical aspects to consider for improving your skill level. Your stance, footwork, striking and defense techniques, and ability to use counterattacks are all essential to become an effective sparring partner. By developing these technical aspects, you will become a better boxer, gain more confidence, and get the most out of your training.

Expert Tips to Improve Your Sparring Game

Anyone who has sparred knows it's not merely about throwing punches. You must be strategic and learn to move correctly to win a sparring match. Here are a few expert tips to help you improve your sparring game and get ahead of your opponents. From peek-a-boo style to timing and distance control, these tips will help you become a better and more effective fighter.

Peek-a-Boo Style

One of the most popular and effective styles in boxing is the peek-a-boo style. A high guard and a bobbing and weaving motion characterize this style. Keeping your arms up high protects your face while weaving in and out, making it difficult for your opponent to hit you. To practice the peek-a-boo style, you should focus on keeping your chin down, with your elbows tucked in and your upper body relaxed. You can practice weaving while throwing punches to keep your opponent guessing and creating openings for counterattacks.

Head Movement and Footwork

Another critical aspect of sparring is head movement and footwork. Learning to move your head and feet in unison helps you dodge your opponent's punches and create openings for your attacks. Keep your feet shoulder-width apart and your weight evenly distributed, ready to move in any direction. Moving your head side-to-side helps you avoid punches; pivoting on your back foot helps you move quickly to the side and escape danger.

Timing and Distance Control

Timing and distance control are vital to any sparring session. Controlling the distance between you and your opponent is crucial. Anticipate your opponent's moves by analyzing his movements and patterns to improve your timing. Practice reacting quickly to his movements by shadowboxing or practicing with a partner.

For distance control, you should get in and out of range quickly while keeping your opponent at the end of your punch. Use footwork to move in and out of range, and learn to throw a punch while moving. The more control you have over the distance, the more effective you'll be in sparring.

Mental Preparation

Sparring is not only about physical strength and technique but also about mental preparation. Going into a sparring session with a clear and focused mindset helps you stay calm and make better decisions. Learn to breathe deeply and focus on the task. Don't let your emotions take over, but instead, use them to fuel your movements and keep you driven.

Consistent Training

Practicing consistently is vital to becoming a better fighter and gaining the confidence to master a discipline. Find a sparring partner you can trust and work with them regularly. Also, pay attention to your technique, focus on proper form, and get feedback from your coach. The more you practice, the better boxer you will become.

Honing Reflexes

Reflexes are essential to successful sparring. As a boxer, you need to have offensive and defensive reactions. The more reflexive you are, the better fighter you will become. You can hone your reflexes by practicing drills involving quick reactions to punches or movements from your opponent. Look at sparring as a way to practice and test your limits in a safe environment. It is not about winning or losing but learning and developing as a boxer.

Ready, Set, Spar! Preparing for Your First Sparring Match

Stepping into the ring for your first sparring match can be intimidating. You're facing an opponent who's actively trying to strike you. It can be nerve-wracking. But with the proper preparation, you can confidently approach your first sparring match. Whether it's your first time or your hundredth, practice is critical. Here are some tips and guidelines to help you prepare for your first sparring match.

Training

Training is the foundation of any successful sparring match. So, before stepping into the ring, ensure you regularly engage in exercises that build your endurance, strength, agility, and balance. Your training should include shadowboxing, bag work, and partner drills. All of which will help you hone your technique and reaction time.

Safety Gear

Safety should be the top priority. Invest in high-quality safety gear to protect your head, mouth, and hands. If you're doing kickboxing, you should also have protective equipment for your shins and feet. Keep your gear clean and in good condition, and replace it when necessary.

Know the Rules

Different martial arts have specific rules for sparring matches, so ensure you know what to expect before entering the ring. For example, familiarize yourself with the points system, the match duration, and the strikes allowed. You should also know what protective gear to wear; this knowledge will help you have a safe and enjoyable sparring experience.

Be Mindful of Your Opponent

Your opponent is your best teacher, so pay attention to how they move in the ring and learn from their techniques. Respect your opponent's physical and emotional boundaries, and always show courtesy. Use the sparring match as an opportunity to build a relationship with your opponent, as they can give you valuable feedback and constructive criticism.

Focus on Footwork

Footwork is often overlooked in training but is crucial for a successful sparring match. Your footwork will help you avoid incoming strikes, keep your balance, and set up counterattacks. So, include footwork drills in your training routine, and practice moving in and out of range.

Master Your Punches

Your punches are your most potent weapons in the ring. You must practice throwing different punches with proper form. Pay attention to your technique and power. You want to ensure you can deliver accurate, powerful punches while controlling your body movements. Test your jabs, crosses, hooks, and uppercuts in sparring matches to see how they work against opponents.

Pick Your Opponents Wisely

When you're sparring, it's essential to find a suitable partner. You need someone who can challenge you and help push your skills to the next level. Working with someone with similar experience may be best if you're a beginner. If you're more experienced, find someone who can challenge you and help you refine your techniques. However, ask your coach for advice if you need help deciding who to choose.

Carry Yourself Confidently

Your mindset is as important as your physical preparation for a sparring match. Before stepping into the ring, focus on positive thoughts and visualize your success. Carry yourself confidently and remember why you're doing this in the first place. Have fun, stay relaxed, and trust in your training and instincts.

Visualize Success

Visualization is a powerful tool for athletes and can help you prepare for the rigors of your first sparring match. Spend time visualizing yourself successfully executing your techniques, dodging your opponent's attacks, and coming out on top. Stay positive, believe in yourself, and remember that sparring is as much a mental challenge as a physical one.

Sparring can be a challenging and rewarding experience, and it's natural to feel nervous before your first match. But with the right mindset and preparation, you can confidently approach your sparring match. Focus on your training, invest in safety gear, familiarize yourself with the rules, prioritize your footwork, and stay positive. By following these tips, you'll be well on your way to success in the ring. Happy sparring.

Chapter 9: Hacking the Heavy Bag

It's no secret that boxing is an intense workout challenging physical and mental resilience. But have you ever tried hacking the heavy bag to take your fitness game to the next level? This workout hack will push you to unleash every ounce of strength you possess. High-intensity training entails throwing punches and kicks on the heavy bag rhythmically and continuously. This workout challenges many muscles, forcing you to engage your core, legs, arms, and shoulders.

When you get the moves right, you'll feel like a champ as you punch and kick your way through the bag, leaving everything out on the mat. This chapter enlightens you about the benefits of training with a heavy bag, what materials you need to get started, and drills to help you perfect your technique. So, grab your gloves, put on your game face, and begin hacking that bag. It's time to unleash the power within.

Punch Your Way to Fitness: Benefits of Training with a Heavy Bag

A heavy bag can help you improve coordination and balance.
https://unsplash.com/photos/5Ua3axiD0kA?utm_source=unsplash&utm_medium=referral&utm_content=creditShareLink

Besides being a means of self-defense, boxing training provides an exceptional full-body workout. A heavy boxing bag for exercise is a great way to get fit, build strength and endurance, and improve overall coordination and balance. So, if you want to level up your fitness routine, let's dive into the benefits of training with a heavy boxing bag.

Total-Body Workout

Bag boxing is a great way to shed off those extra pounds and work toward building a lean and toned physique. Punching, kicking, and dodging movements engage your entire body and activate multiple muscle groups. In addition, throwing high-intensity combinations forces your body to exert a lot of energy and burn calories. Throw various punches and movements, and remember to keep your core engaged throughout the exercise to get the most out of your workout.

Improved Cardiovascular Endurance

Boxing bag training is excellent for improving your cardiovascular endurance. The continuous movement of your body while engaging in different punching combinations adds a significant challenge to your heart and lungs. The increased heart rate during training helps build better endurance, stamina, and cardiovascular health. Gradually increasing the intensity and incorporating high-intensity interval training (HIIT) into your workout routine helps you achieve optimal fitness.

Increased Strength and Power

The weight of the boxing bag ranges from 70-100 pounds, meaning you engage your upper and lower body muscles and work toward developing stronger punches, kicks, and overall strength. In addition, the resistance training aspect of bag boxing helps you build muscle and increase your general power. This training can be especially beneficial for athletes like wrestlers and football players, as it improves their power, speed, and explosiveness.

Improved Footwork and Balance

Your footwork and balance are crucial in boxing. Without proper footwork and balance, you risk losing control of your punches, leaving yourself vulnerable to attacks. By training with a heavy boxing bag, you learn various footwork techniques, improve your balance, and better understand how to shift your weight during boxing combinations. In addition, incorporating shadowboxing and lateral movements into your workout improves your overall footwork and balance.

Better Accuracy and Timing

Bag boxing allows you to work on your accuracy by throwing punches and aiming for specific points on the bag. This training improves your timing and reaction by mimicking sparring conditions. Throwing quick and precise combinations improves hand-eye coordination, making it easier to respond quickly to punches.

Warm-Up Exercises

Boxing is one of the most intense and physically demanding workouts. It requires strength and endurance, along with proper technique and form. Therefore, before you start training with a heavy boxing bag, you must do warm-up exercises to get your body ready for the rigors of the workout. This section discusses the benefits of pre-workout warm-up exercises and explores five activities to prepare your body for an intense boxing workout.

Jumping Jacks

Jumping Jacks are a classic warm-up exercise, and for a good reason – they are an efficient way to get your heart rate up and blood flowing throughout your body. Start with your feet together and your arms at your sides. Then jump, spreading your legs apart while raising your arms out to the side until your hands meet above your head. Return to the starting position and repeat. Do this for about a minute or until your heart rate is up.

High Knees

High Knees are another warm-up exercise to increase your heart rate and blood circulation. Stand with your feet hip-width apart. Then, raise your right leg, driving your knee toward your chest. As you lower your right leg, lift your left leg similarly, alternating legs quickly while standing in place. Do this for about a minute or until you feel warmed up.

Arm Circles

Arm circles prepare your upper body for the workout. Stand with your feet shoulder-width apart with your arms straight out at your sides, parallel to the floor. Make small circles with your arms and gradually increase the size of the circles until you are making large circles with your entire arm. After completing a set in one direction, reverse the direction and repeat. Do this for about 30 seconds in each direction.

Leg Swings

Leg Swings are an excellent warm-up exercise. Stand next to a wall or pole to maintain your balance. Then swing your right leg forward and backward as far as it comfortably goes while keeping your upper body still. After completing a set with one leg, repeat with the other leg. Do this for about ten swings on each leg.

Dynamic Stretches

Dynamic stretches involve movement with controlled momentum and improve flexibility and range of motion. Start with a lunge and transition to a hamstring stretch by straightening your front leg while leaning forward. Then return to the lunge position and transition to a quad stretch by bending your back leg while bringing your heel towards your buttocks. Repeat this movement for 5-10 reps before switching legs.

Training with a heavy boxing bag is highly beneficial for your overall fitness, but it also puts a lot of stress on your body if you don't do it right. Adding these warm-up exercises to your boxing routine reduces the risk of injury and increases your performance. Always warm up before a workout and make it a regular part of your routine to ensure you get the most out of your training.

Basic Heavy Bag Drills: The Building Blocks of Boxing

Boxing is not only about punching hard and knocking out your opponent–it's a skill requiring discipline and consistent training. One of the best ways to improve your boxing skills is by incorporating regular heavy bag drills into your routine. Heavy bag drills help boxers of all skill levels build endurance, improve technique, and increase strength. This section discusses basic heavy bag drills every fighter should learn to master.

Jabs and Crosses

The jab is a basic punch in boxing. It's efficient and sets up other punches. To execute a basic jab-heavy bag drill, do the following:

1. Start by standing in front of the bag with your feet shoulder-width apart and your dominant foot slightly behind the other.

2. Place your lead hand near the bag, and extend your arm, making a quick, snappy punch.

3. After the jab, step back and follow it up with a cross to the bag.

The cross is a straight punch with your dominant hand to follow the jab. Jab-cross combination heavy bag drills are great for warming up and perfecting techniques.

Uppercuts and Hooks

Uppercuts and hooks are punches meant to be thrown at close range. First, stand close to the bag with your knees slightly bent to execute an uppercut-heavy bag drill. Then, bend your arm and use your body weight to throw the punch upward toward the bag. On the other hand, hooks use your body's rotational power to throw a punch from the side toward the bag. Hook-heavy bag drills are perfect for working on body mechanics. Practice on both sides to ensure you have equal strength in both arms.

Body Combinations

Body combinations are a vital pillar of boxing training. These combos work the entire body and get the boxer moving around the bag. Body combination-heavy bag drills include movements like body jabs, body hooks, and body crosses, targeting the opponent's torso. Mix and match these combinations to create endless exercises to improve your boxing technique.

Footwork Drills

Footwork drills improve your foot speed, agility, and balance. An excellent footwork drill for beginners is the "Step and Pivot." Stand in your basic boxing stance, take a small step with your lead foot, then pivot on the ball of your foot to turn your body. Repeat the drill by following up with a punch or a combination. This drill helps with stability and balance.

Fill the Bag Drills

"Fill the bag" drills are when you use the entire upper and lower body to hit the bag as hard as possible. Begin a fill-the-bag exercise with a round of combination punches. Follow it up with a series of aggressive jabs, crosses, uppercuts, and hooks. This drill builds confidence and is a great way to push yourself to keep your energy levels up.

Get Your Sweat On: A Guide to Heavy Bag Drills

Not only is it a great way to relieve stress and release pent-up frustrations, but training with a heavy bag is also a fantastic way to improve your physical health. Professional boxers and MMA fighters use the serious bag workout to improve their strength, power, and endurance. But don't let that intimidate you. Here are simple drills to follow for a great heavy bag workout:

Rounds 1-3: Basic Punches

The first three rounds of your workout should focus on perfecting the basics: jabs, crosses, and hooks. These three punches allow you to establish a rhythm, getting a feel for the bag and the impact you're generating. Next, focus on a proper technique. For example, move from the hips, twist your shoulders, and imagine your target in front of you. This works your upper body and core muscles. Each round should be 1-2 minutes, and you must maintain a steady pace. Consider taking a 30-to-60-second rest between rounds.

Round 4: Fill the Bag

Now it's time to let out some of that pent-up frustration. For this round, focus on hitting the bag with as much rage and power as possible. As you strike the bag, pick up the pace and throw the combination you've just worked on. Keep this up for a complete round of two minutes, then rest for 30 seconds. Repeat this for two to three rounds, keeping up that intensity.

Round 5: Footwork Drills

The fifth round is all about footwork. Play some of your favorite tunes and circle the bag with different combinations of step-by-step movements. You can shuffle around the bag in different directions. For instance, start by stepping left, then as you move around the bag entirely, start with the combination moving to the right. Again, you get a significant drill in improving your footwork and core strength while burning calories.

Rounds 6-8: Body Combinations

Use these three rounds to focus on hitting the bag with combinations using your upper and lower body. Body combinations should be the primary focus of this round. Remember, the power comes from your hips. So, keep moving them and switch between throwing punches from both sides of the body. Each round should last two minutes, with a minute rest in between. These rounds work your entire body, not only the arms.

Rounds 9-15: Jabs, Crosses, and Hooks

In the last few rounds, focus on short bursts of high-intensity action, with short rest periods between rounds. Perform a series of jabs, crosses, and hooks on the heavy bags, maintaining that rhythm you worked on during the first three rounds. Add power to each combination and feel the impact of every punch. Repeat these rounds one, two, or three times, taking a 30-second rest between each round.

Cool Down Exercises after a Heavy Bag Workout

If you've ever taken a kickboxing or boxing class, you know how intense a heavy-bag workout can be. The punching, kicking, and footwork require much energy and exertion. After an intense workout, it's essential to take a few minutes to cool down and properly stretch your muscles. This section discusses practical cool-down exercises to avoid injury and recover from your heavy bag workout.

Calf Stretches

Calves are one of the areas that can become stiff and sore after a heavy bag workout. To properly stretch them out, stand facing a wall about an arm's length away. Place your palms on the wall and step with one foot back, keeping it flat on the ground. Lean into the wall until you feel a stretch in the calf of the back leg. Hold the stretch for 15-30 seconds, then switch legs. Repeat this stretch a few times on both sides.

Quadriceps Stretches

The quadriceps, or front thigh muscles, also work heavily during a heavy bag workout. First, stand with your feet hip-distance apart and bend one knee, bringing your heel towards your glutes. Next, grasp your ankle and gently pull it toward your glutes, feeling a stretch in your quadriceps. Hold the stretch for 15-30 seconds, then switch legs. Repeat this stretch on both sides a few times.

Glute Stretches

The glutes, or butt muscles, are frequently used during a heavy bag workout. To stretch them out, do the following:

1. Lie on your back with your knees bent and feet flat on the ground.
2. Cross your left ankle over your right knee, grab your right thigh, and gently pull your leg towards your chest. You should feel a stretch in your left glute.
3. Hold the stretch for 15-30 seconds, then switch legs.
4. Repeat this stretch a few times on both sides.

Neck and Shoulder Stretches

Carrying tension in the neck and shoulders is common, especially after a heavy bag workout. Sit or stand straight and slowly roll your head from side to side, bringing your ear toward your shoulder to release this tension. Take your time; don't force the stretch. Next, shrug your shoulders toward your ears, hold for a few seconds, then release. Repeat these stretches a few times.

Yoga Poses

Yoga poses are excellent for stretching your entire body and promoting relaxation after a heavy bag workout. Beneficial poses include downward-facing dog, child's pose, and cat-cow pose. As you move through these poses, focus on your breath and release muscle tension.

Taking a few minutes to cool down and stretch after a heavy-bag workout significantly affects how you feel the next day. Incorporating calf stretches, quadriceps stretches, glute stretches, neck and shoulder stretches, and yoga poses into your post-workout routine can prevent injury and promote muscle recovery. Always listen to your body, and don't push yourself too hard when stretching.

A heavy bag workout is excellent for working your entire body and relieving stress. While the training might seem intimidating, now that you know what to do, it's easier than ever to get started. Follow the guidelines above, and soon enough, you'll be an expert. Remember, the key to the heavy bag workout is to focus on technique and power, so take time to perfect your form and keep pushing yourself. You will soon see results and power punches.

Chapter 10: Twenty Common Mistakes to Avoid (Rookie or Not)

Boxing is daunting, especially with the high stakes of fighting against an opponent and the pressure to win. As with any skill, mistakes are bound to happen, whether a seasoned pro or a beginner. However, errors can be turned into opportunities for growth and improvement. The key is learning from them, adjusting your technique, and pushing forward. So, whether you've accidentally dropped your guard or thrown a wild punch, don't be too hard on yourself. Instead, please take it as a chance to improve and keep slugging it out in the ring.

This chapter examines some of the most common mistakes beginner and even advanced boxers make, why they're wrong, and how to avoid or correct them. Everything from incorrect breathing to not taking breaks is covered. These are issues you want to avoid if you're serious about being a better boxer. The best fighters learn from their mistakes and continually strive to improve.

Common Mistakes Beginner Boxers Make

It takes a lot of effort and time to master the required skills and boxing techniques. However, as a beginner, you must avoid common mistakes that could harm your training and progress. This section explains common mistakes beginner boxers make, why they are wrong, and how to avoid and correct them.

Not Warming Up Properly

A warm-up is necessary for any sport.

Warming up is essential in any workout, including boxing. However, some beginner boxers don't give it the attention it deserves. A proper warm-up prepares your body and mind for the intense training ahead and prevents injuries. Skipping the warm-up can lead to muscle strains and soreness, delaying your progress or even ending your career.

Spend 10-15 minutes warming up before you start training to avoid this mistake. A good warm-up should include cardiovascular exercises (jumping jacks or jump rope), joint mobilization exercises (leg swings or arm circles), and dynamic stretching exercises (such as lunges or squats). Also, cool down and stretch after your training session to help your body recover and prevent soreness.

Not Using the Proper Technique

Having the proper technique is crucial in boxing. With the wrong approach, you risk injuring yourself or your opponent. Unfortunately, many beginner boxers neglect to focus on the proper technique because they think it's unimportant. Yet, it is the foundation of everything you do in boxing. Learn the appropriate technique for each punch to avoid this mistake. First, work on the basics, like footwork, stance, and head movement, before moving on to advanced techniques. Next, practice each punch, focusing on the correct form and movement. Also, consider hiring a coach or a mentor to guide you through the technical aspects of boxing.

Not Eating the Right Foods

Boxing requires a lot of energy and stamina, so you must fuel your body correctly. However, some beginner boxers don't pay enough attention to their nutrition, thinking it's unnecessary. Wrong. Eating the right foods will significantly impact your performance and progress.

To avoid this mistake, do the following:

1. Ensure a balanced and healthy diet, including carbohydrates, proteins, and fats.
2. In addition, eat plenty of fruits and vegetables, which provide essential vitamins and minerals.
3. Avoid eating junk and processed food, which can harm your body and negatively affect your performance.
4. Drink enough water to keep your body hydrated.

Not Anticipating Your Opponent's Movements

In boxing, you must anticipate your opponent's movements to counter them. Unfortunately, many beginner boxers don't consider this, leaving them vulnerable to attack. However, most opponents are experienced, so they may sense your lack of preparation and take advantage.

To avoid this mistake, do the following:

1. Stay on your toes and pay attention to your opponent's body language.
2. Learn to read their movements to predict what they will do next.
3. Practice counter-punching drills with a partner to help you develop good reflexes and anticipation skills.

Not Following the 3-Second Rule

The 3-second rule is a classic boxing strategy that's been around for many years. It states that you should take 3 seconds to think and plan your next move after a punch has been thrown. It is important because it allows you to assess the situation, develop a strategy, and carry it out. Unfortunately, some beginner boxers don't follow this rule, leading to hasty and ill-advised moves.

To avoid this mistake, do the following:

1. Take a few seconds to think before you act.
2. Focus on your breathing and clear your head.
3. Analyze the situation and decide.

Practicing this rule in drills with a partner would be best to help you develop a better sense of timing.

Not Working on Footwork

Footwork is essential to being a successful boxer. Unfortunately, many beginners neglect this aspect of their training and suffer the consequences. Good footwork enables fighters to move efficiently around the ring, avoid punches, and land their own. Therefore, beginner boxers should focus on developing footwork drills into their training routine to improve their agility, coordination, and balance.

Not Focusing on Defense

Defense is equally as important as offense in boxing. Unfortunately, many beginners only focus on landing punches instead of their security, leaving them vulnerable to their opponent's attacks. Good defense allows a boxer to block, slip, duck, or weave to avoid punches and counterattack effectively. Beginner boxers should incorporate defensive drills into their training routine to hone these skills, including practicing blocking punches, slipping, and moving their head.

Incorrect Breathing

Boxers need to learn to breathe correctly during training and fights. Many beginners do not control their breathing, causing them to lose energy and oxygen supply to their muscles, resulting in exhaustion and poor performance. Boxers must learn to breathe deeply and regulate their breathing during training to improve their stamina and endurance.

Not Focusing on Strength and Conditioning

Boxing requires a high level of strength and conditioning to be successful. Unfortunately, many beginners focus more on boxing drills and neglect their overall strength and conditioning. Building and maintaining power and conditioning through weight training, cardio exercises, and other conditioning drills will make any boxer more effective in the ring. Combining strength and conditioning exercises improves performance and takes your boxing to the next level.

Not Stretching Enough

Stretching before training is essential for preventing injuries and increasing flexibility and range of motion. Sadly, some beginner boxers skip stretching or do it minimally. Not stretching enough can lead to muscle strains and tears, significantly impacting the training's progress. Schedule sufficient time for stretching before each training session to avoid this mistake. Start with simple stretches, like neck rotations, arm circles, and trunk twists. Then, gradually work up to more advanced stretches, like splits, back bends, and hip openers.

Not Staying Hydrated

Boxing is a high-intensity workout making you sweat profusely, leading to dehydration if you don't replenish lost fluids. Not staying hydrated leads to tiredness, dizziness, and cramping. In addition, it significantly affects your stamina and performance during training. Drink plenty of fluids before, during, and after training sessions to avoid this mistake. Keep a bottle of water nearby and sip regularly to stay hydrated. *Avoid sugary drinks or drinks with caffeine, as they can lead to dehydration.*

Over-Relying on Upper Body Strength

Boxing is not solely about upper body strength. Your lower body, core, and coordination are significant and dictate how you box. Unfortunately, many beginners make the mistake of focusing too much on upper body strength, leading to muscle imbalances, poor form, and fatigue. Incorporate lower body and core exercises into your workout routine to avoid this mistake. Examples of lower-body exercises include squats, lunges, and jumping rope. Core exercises can consist of planks, Russian twists, and sit-ups.

Poor Footwork

Boxing is a sport requiring excellent footwork. However, beginners don't pay more attention to the importance of footwork, leading to several mistakes, including improper balance, poor movement, and susceptibility to injuries. To avoid this mistake, focus on improving your footwork by practicing footwork drills, like shadowboxing, ladder drills, and pivots. In addition, work on your reaction time and coordination by doing exercises like jump squats, hurdle jumps, and burpees.

Training too Hard

While it is essential to train hard, overtraining can lead to burnout, injury, and fatigue. Beginners often make the mistake of training too hard or too frequently, leading to a lack of progress in the long run. Establish a regular training schedule and include rest days to avoid this mistake. Work on gradually increasing the intensity of your workouts while listening to your body and not pushing yourself to exhaustion.

Not Working on Punch Speed

One of the common mistakes beginner boxers make is not working on their punch speed. Your punch speed is crucial in boxing; neglecting it can cost you the fight. Include speed drills in your training routine to avoid this mistake. Practice shadowboxing, speed bag drills, and double-end bag drills to improve your punch speed. Another way to improve your punch speed is to work on your footwork. Proper footwork enables you to move quickly and punch faster. Learn the proper boxing stance and footwork to improve your speed.

Not Keeping Balance

Beginner boxers often overlook the importance of balance in boxing. Keeping your balance is crucial. It allows you to move quickly and dodge punches. Not keeping balance makes you an easy target for your opponent. Practice balance exercises specific to boxing to avoid this mistake. Practice moving around the ring, shifting your weight, and pivoting on your feet. Regularly practicing these exercises will help you to maintain your balance during your fights.

Not Relaxing During Rounds

One of the common mistakes beginner boxers make is not relaxing during rounds. Boxing requires a lot of energy, and you must conserve it during games. Tensing up drains your energy and tires you quickly. Practice breathing exercises during your training sessions to avoid this mistake. For example, take deep breaths and exhale slowly to relax your muscles. Also, focus on your technique instead of the outcome to conserve your energy and stay relaxed during your rounds.

Lack of Mental Strength

One of the biggest mistakes beginner boxers make is underestimating the importance of mental strength. Boxing is a mentally demanding sport, and your ability to stay focused and determined is as important as your physical skills. When you don't have mental strength, you might struggle to push yourself in training and shrink in the face of pressure during a fight. Working on your mental strength is essential. Set achievable goals, visualize success, and stay positive and focused during training to avoid this mistake. You can also work with a coach or sports psychologist to help you develop mental toughness.

Not Having a Good Workout Routine

Another mistake beginner boxers make is not maintaining a consistent and well-rounded workout routine. Fighters need strength, endurance, and agility, but you'll be disadvantaged in the ring if you only focus on one area. Developing a comprehensive workout routine that includes strength training, cardio, and agility drills is important to avoid this mistake. It's essential to vary your workouts to prevent hitting a plateau. Working with a personal trainer or coach can help you create a customized workout plan that caters to your specific needs and goals.

Not Taking Breaks

Many beginner boxers fall victim to overtraining. They think the more training they do, the faster they'll improve. However, overtraining can lead to injuries, burnout, and plateauing. Taking regular breaks and rest days is crucial to avoid this mistake. Rest allows your muscles to recover and repair, reducing the risk of injury and preventing burnout. Listening to your body and accordingly adjusting your training schedule is important. If you feel exhausted or sore, take an extra day off to recover.

Boxing is an intense sport requiring discipline, focus, and hard work. As a beginner, it is essential to avoid these common mistakes to prevent injuries and make consistent progress. Taking the time to stretch, staying hydrated, focusing on whole-body strength and footwork, and finding a balance between hard work and rest are crucial to becoming a successful boxer.

Overall, becoming a successful boxer takes more than just punching hard. It is imperative to be mentally tough, have a comprehensive workout routine, and take regular breaks. By working on your punch speed, keeping your balance, and relaxing during your rounds, you'll improve your boxing skills and avoid making costly mistakes. Remember, success in boxing is a journey, and the path to success often requires patience and persistence. Follow these tips, and you'll be well on your way to becoming a successful boxer.

Conclusion

Boxing is an intense and captivating sport that has been around for centuries. From its humble beginnings to the spectacular world championships we see today, boxing has captivated audiences with its skill, speed, and power. In this ultimate boxing guide, you explored everything about getting started with boxing, from the basics of the sport to advanced techniques and drills. This easy-to-understand guide explored how the sport evolved and gained international popularity from ancient Greece to today. It touched on the different modern boxing styles, from amateur to professional leagues, and the various weight classes and rules that apply.

Boxing is a great way to stay fit, improve coordination, and release steam. But if you want to step into the ring, you must know the most basic rules and regulations of boxing. Firstly, you need a sturdy pair of boxing gloves to protect your hands from injury and to pack a punch. A heavy bag is another essential piece of equipment for practicing jabs, hooks, and uppercuts. Hand wraps help support your wrist and prevent injury, and a mouthguard is crucial for protecting your teeth and jaw. Finally, comfortable and durable boxing shoes provide the necessary support and traction in the ring. With this essential equipment in your kit, you are ready to start throwing punches like a pro.

You must understand the importance of your stance, guard, and footwork to be a successful boxer. These three elements are the boxing technique's foundation and can make or break your performance in the ring. Mastering the right stance helps you maintain balance and stability, while a solid guard protects you from your opponent's punches. Footwork is essential to keep you on your feet, ready to move in any direction.

This guide focused on the different punches and counterpunches in boxing, illustrating the jab, the straight, the hook, the uppercut, and how to throw them correctly. It covered some of the most effective counterpunches used to gain an advantage in the ring. However, you will always need a solid defense to become a successful boxer, regardless of how good your offense is. This book discussed the most effective defense techniques in boxing. In addition, it discussed the importance of distance control, how to slip and block punches, and using your guard to avoid getting hit.

This ultimate boxing guide has given you an excellent overview of the sport and everything you need to get started with boxing. From the sport's history to the Peek-A-Boo technique, it explored a wide range of topics and provided valuable insight and tips. Remember, boxing is a highly skilled and demanding sport requiring plenty of dedication, discipline, and training to master. So, whether you are a newbie or an experienced pro, use this guide as a foundation to build your skills and become the best boxer you can be.

Here's another book by Clint Sharp that you might like

CLINT SHARP

Brazilian Jiu-Jitsu

A COMPREHENSIVE GUIDE TO BJJ
GRAPPLING BASICS FOR BEGINNERS AND
A COMPARISON WITH JAPANESE JUJITSU

References

(N.d.). Realbuzz.com. https://www.realbuzz.com/articles-interests/sports-activities/article/the-basic-skills-of-boxing/

Chen, L. (2021, June 15). The ultimate boxing workout for beginners. Byrdie. https://www.byrdie.com/boxing-workouts-5188633

Duquette, T. (2021, April 13). How to box at home - techniques for beginners. Joinfightcamp.com; FightCamp. https://blog.joinfightcamp.com/training/5-basic-boxing-techniques-to-learn-at-home-during-quarantine/

Evolve, M. M. A. (2022, October 2). 15 basic boxing combinations you should master first. Evolve Daily. https://evolve-mma.com/blog/15-basic-boxing-combinations-you-should-master-first/

Imre, B. (2020, August 14). 6 basic boxing punches & how to throw them correctly. PunchingBagsGuide. https://punchingbagsguide.com/basic-boxing-punches-guide/

Johnny, N. (2012, November 23). The BEGINNER'S guide to boxing. How to Box | ExpertBoxing. https://expertboxing.com/the-beginners-guide-to-boxing

Mahoney, K. (2020, May 2). 7 boxing fundamentals everyone should know. Muscle & Fitness. https://www.muscleandfitness.com/muscle-fitness-hers/hers-workouts/basics-boxing/

McNulty, R. (2020, May 29). The beginner's guide to boxing training. Muscle & Fitness. https://www.muscleandfitness.com/workouts/workout-tips/the-beginners-guide-to-boxing-training/

Ritterbeck, M. (2017, April 11). Boxing for beginners: Boxing basics for stance, breath, and punches. Greatist. https://greatist.com/fitness/boxing-workout-basic-moves-for-beginners